THE UNLIKELY WORLD OF THE MONTGOMERY BUS BOYCOTT

THE UNLIKELY WORLD OF THE MONTGOMERY BUS BOYCOTT

Solidarity Across Alabama, the United Kingdom, and South Africa

COLE S. MANLEY

NEWSOUTH BOOKS

Montgomery

NewSouth Books
105 S. Court Street
Montgomery, AL 36104

Cataloging-in-Publication Data
The Unlikely World of the Montgomery Bus Boycott:
Solidarity Across Alabama, the United Kingdom, and South Africa
Author: Cole Manley
ISBN 978-1-58838-452-2 (trade paper)
ISBN 978-1-58838-453-9 (ebook)

Design by Randall Williams

Printed in the United States of America

*The Black Belt, defined by its dark, rich soil, stretches across central
Alabama. It was the heart of the cotton belt. It was and is a place of
great beauty, of extreme wealth and grinding poverty, of pain and joy.
Here we take our stand, listening to the past, looking to the future.*

For my parents,
John Manley and Kathy Sharp

Contents

Abbreviations

| *Archives*

ADAH – Alabama Department of Archives and History

ASU – Alabama State University Archives and Special Collections

ARC – Amistad Research Center

BA – Bristol Archives

MLKI – Martin Luther King, Jr. Research and Education Institute, Stanford University, CA

SC – Schomburg Center for Research in Black Culture

SCPC – Swarthmore College Peace Collection

| *Organizations*

ASC – Alabama State College

BOC – Bristol Omnibus Company

FOR – Fellowship of Reconciliation

IRR – Institute of Race Relations

MIA – Montgomery Improvement Association

NAACP – National Association for the Advancement of Colored People

SNCC – Student Nonviolent Coordinating Committee

TGWU – Transport and General Workers' Union

TU – Tuskegee University

WIDC – West Indian Development Council

WPC – Women's Political Council

Preface

When I think about the historical significance of the Montgomery Bus Boycott, I remember the life of John Lewis. Growing up in the rural area near Troy, Alabama, an hour's drive from Montgomery, Lewis came across stories about the boycott in the local newspaper his grandfather gave him. References to Rosa Parks and Martin Luther King Jr. stoked Lewis's curiosity. Like King, Lewis was inspired by oratory and by the social gospel. Having listened to King's sermons on the radio in 1955, Lewis, without a congregation, preached to anyone who would listen, whether to his family or his family's chickens.[1] Lewis recalled in 2020 that "the action of Rosa Parks and the words of Dr. King inspired me . . . and I kept saying to myself, 'If something can happen like this in Montgomery, why can't we change Troy?'"[2] Lewis's question is at the heart of this book. A similar question would be asked by people reading about the Montgomery boycott in cities and towns across the country and around the world, as Black South Africans, White pacifists, and West Indians in the United Kingdom wondered how this small city in Alabama might influence their own freedom struggles.

In the case of the Montgomery boycott, I am convinced that the movement and its reverberations through time and space continue to influence domestic politics and generate new solidarities internationally. I hope that you may understand some of my conclusions about how and why.

This project began as a master's thesis when I was a student at Columbia University, but its roots extend much deeper. In high school, my inspirational history teacher, Cathy Schager, introduced me to King's writings, including his famous "Letter from Birmingham Jail." A few years later, my mentor at Stanford University, Dr. Clayborne Carson, taught me that the social movements of the post-World War II era were not simply struggles for civil rights but represented a tapestry of protests for economic and racial justice. As Dr. Carson's research assistant at the Martin Luther King, Jr. Research and Education Institute—which has published King's writings in a planned fourteen-volume series—I helped produce an innovative online course on King's inner life and global vision. The course illustrated how the Black struggle for freedom in the United States connected to anticolonial and independence struggles around the world.

Studying the movements of the 1950s and 1960s inspired me to become involved in student organizing. As police killings sparked protests that would become known as the Black Lives Matter movement, I joined in marches across the Stanford campus. My education reading about mass movements one night and participating in student movements the next day taught me about the collective power of nonviolent struggles for freedom.

To understand the movements of the 1950s and 1960s, we must consider how organizers thought about themselves on a local and global scale. Transnational history, which the historian Lara Putnam defines as "seeing connections across borders and taking seriously both the connections and the borders," has been a focus of scholarship since at least the late 1990s.[3] This movement among historians considering national and international phenomena has more recently faced challenges due to the staying power of nationalism. The rise of fascism and white supremacy, while transnational ideologies themselves, have nonetheless highlighted how nations remain significant historical forces. This work does not dispute the power of national borders, but it does suggest another powerful force influencing national and international politics: the movements across borders and oceans that looked beyond a single nation to create new solidarities in the struggle for freedom.

I believe that this project is timely and relevant for "New South" history. The New South movement, known to many through the historian C. Vann Woodward and his seminal book *Origins of the New South*, has changed over time to reflect social and political realities.[4] Today, New South history responds to the Black Lives Matter movement and the Montgomery Bus Boycott is a bridge between current organizing and the movements of the post-World War II era.

Through their attention to Gandhian nonviolence and anticolonialism, Montgomery activists signaled their global awareness. Similarly, Black Lives Matter activists have connected the struggle against police brutality to economic justice, to freedom struggles in the Middle East, and towards providing healthcare, jobs, and housing for all people. Just as the "civil rights" movement was never solely concerned with constitutional rights, today's activists embrace the intersections between economic, social, and racial justice, even as they target specific policy changes.

As with all projects, some limits must be placed on research and writing. I focused on one main case study: the Bristol, England, bus boycott in 1963. An article by the historian Nick Juravich— "A Black Englishman in the Heart of the Confederacy: The Transnational Life of Paul Stephenson"—turned my attention towards this boycott.[5] I began thinking about how protest movements in the South connected to struggles for racial justice in the United Kingdom. Meetings with Columbia University librarian John Tofanelli helped me locate archives and primary sources.

I focused on the Montgomery boycott in part because of Stephenson's life story. Like John Lewis, Stephenson had been inspired by Rosa Parks's action, so much so that during protests in Bristol he had a colleague pose for a picture at the back of a bus in homage to the struggle for freedom in Alabama. I wondered what national or international struggles inspired the Montgomery boycott. My advisors at Columbia, especially Professor Frank Guridy, encouraged me to be open to geographic and thematic complexity. Dr. Guridy's course on "Approaches to History" fueled my intellectual desire, and I enjoyed going to his office hours, where he was a kind mentor with helpful suggestions for readings and archives. Professors Barbara Fields, Stephanie McCurry, and Samuel Roberts were also important teachers and advisors, and I deepened my understanding of nineteenth- and twentieth-century United States history through their courses and office hours.

Research for this project included archives in the United States and in the United Kingdom. I first visited the Swarthmore College Peace Collection to analyze the Fellowship of Reconciliation (FOR) records. Archivist Wendy Chmielewski directed me towards materials which provided important links between US-based organizers and UK-based peace activists. The FOR's reach extended to South Africa, where there were numerous connections between the anti-apartheid struggle and the Montgomery boycott. At the Peace Collection I discovered a copy of the comic book, *Martin Luther King. Jr. and the Montgomery Story,* that was read by UK-based FOR organizers and by South African church leaders.

In Montgomery, Alabama, I focused on state and university

archives. I spent days poring over Alabama State's impressive primary sources related to the boycott, and I met local historians and publishers preserving this history, including Randall Williams of NewSouth Books and Professor Derryn Moten at Alabama State. I will always remember the kindness and generosity they showed a young student without many ties to the city. My trip also led to a chance meeting with the Reverend Robert and Jeannie Graetz, who had been among the few Whites in Montgomery to actively support the boycott as it unfolded.

I also visited the Amistad Research Center's collections in New Orleans. Phillip Cunningham, head of Research Services, directed me to the Preston and Bonita Valien collection, which includes first-person observations of mass meetings. This collection preserves the tactical brilliance of Montgomery organizers, who set up a complex carpool system and used mass meetings in churches to form an infrastructure of freedom and resistance.

In September 2019, I moved from New York to London and began the second year of my master's program at the London School of Economics. I arrived in Bristol, in the southwest of England, unsure about what the city's archives would contain about the 1963 protest. Using newspaper articles, I pieced together an incomplete story of the Bristol boycott, one which, unlike the protest in Montgomery, has not been recorded in many primary or secondary sources and remains under-studied in the United Kingdom as a whole. To fill in archival gaps, I used materials from the Institute of Race Relations' archive in London, which contains copies of Claudia Jones's *West Indian Gazette*. Jones's publication contextualized the experiences of West Indian post-World War II migrants to the United Kingdom, including many who arrived in Bristol in the 1950s and 1960s.

There is much more to be learned about the Bristol boycott,

but this work builds on earlier scholarship by situating both the Bristol and Montgomery boycotts within a transnational struggle for freedom and justice. I came to realize after finishing archival research that ties between both boycotts to the anti-apartheid struggle document an important triangular US-UK-South Africa relationship, a social network further complicated by the fact that many Bristol organizers hailed from Jamaica and other parts of the Caribbean. Highlighting ties between these freedom struggles has been a focus of earlier scholarship, but I believe that the Bristol and Montgomery boycotts provide another layer of analysis and investigation for future scholars.[6]

Perhaps historians should be thinking about the post-World War II era as a distinct and special period of radical ferment in all three countries. Scholarship has emphasized connections between the United States and the United Kingdom as Black Power coalesced in the late 1960s, but the records of the FOR, the *West Indian Gazette*, and the Montgomery comic book suggest that longstanding connections were being solidified during the more "conventional" phase of civil rights protest in the 1950s and 1960s.[7]

After completing my master's program, I shared the thesis with Randall Williams, the co-creator of NewSouth Books, with numerous titles on the struggle for freedom in the US South. I was deeply honored when he invited me to publish the project with NewSouth Books. Based in Montgomery, NewSouth has a long track record of publishing extraordinary books, from Lawrence Reddick's *Crusader Without Violence,* the first biography of King, to Fred Gray's *Bus Ride to Justice,* to Robert Graetz's *A White Preacher's Message on Race and Reconciliation,* and many more.

NewSouth is also concerned with how its books are received and with how they influence the world. As Williams has explained, "we believe strongly in the transformative power of information and knowledge, and we hope that the books we publish offer collective insight that helps the region grow toward 'the beloved community' and the fulfillment of the democratic promise."[8]

Mine is one small addition to a voluminous literature on the Montgomery Bus Boycott. If I could have written this twenty or thirty years ago, more oral interviews could have added the vibrancy that comes from personal recollections. The writer and historian David Garrow was kind enough to share transcripts of an oral interview with Jo Ann Robinson that he completed in 1984, and, luckily, Alabama State's and other archives have preserved recorded and transcribed interviews with organizers.

The story proceeds chronologically. I begin with political organizing in Montgomery during the post-World War II period, organizing led by Black women in the Women's Political Council (WPC), and by men and women in the local branch of the National Association for the Advancement of Colored People (NAACP). The history and trajectory of Black organizing networks in Montgomery generated a political climate which made the boycott less surprising in hindsight.

In Part I, I analyze how organizers in Montgomery thought about their movement and its connections to people and ideas beyond the United States. I focus on how Gandhian nonviolence and decolonization influenced the thinking and public messaging of boycott organizers. Moving beyond Montgomery, I emphasize how the boycott came to be known to organizers in other parts of the world, especially in the United Kingdom and South Africa. In part through the aforementioned FOR comic book, the Montgomery boycott came to be known more as King's struggle than as a grassroots undertaking, and King was identified as a Gandhian peace prophet.

In Part II, I analyze the Bristol bus boycott of 1963 as a case study in how organizers in other countries interpreted and remembered the Montgomery boycott. I emphasize the long and tedious negotiations between Bristol leaders and bus company officials that ultimately led to the resolution of the protest, and I highlight the political leaders who pressured the bus company into negotiations.

In my conclusion, I raise questions about how we remember freedom struggles and about the connections between social movements. I do not believe that stories should be entirely removed from the political context in which they are written. In today's political climate, the Montgomery boycott can offer a sobering and inspirational account of what a unified social movement can accomplish.

ACKNOWLEDGMENTS

The Unlikely World is the result of many studies coming together, and so many people contributed to my research, writing, and editing. Professor Frank Guridy sparked my interest in transnational history, while Dr. Line Lillevik and Sarah Wadlinger led a master's program that was both highly organized and intellectually liberating. Professor Stephanie McCurry encouraged me to think about transnational history in the context of nineteenth-century civil wars. At the LSE, Dr. Imaobong Umoren deepened my understanding of transnational politics and Black internationalism in the United Kingdom and the Caribbean.

Haris Durrani provided detailed feedback and suggestions as I edited the thesis for publication. His fabulous imagination has helped me consider new connections between my work and other scholarship. Thank you, as always, for your generosity and friendship; I am excited to see where your writing takes you next. Arthur Braswell, friend and co-worker and fellow co-op resident, provided important feedback on my ideas about United States history and the Cold War political context throughout the project. Professor

Nick Juravich met with me early on and recommended several archives that proved indispensable, among them the Institute of Race Relations (IRR) in London. He also provided helpful suggestions for studying and writing about transnational history.

My friends in the master's program helped workshop the thesis and saw it grow and change. Having such good friends kept me going even as a pandemic forced me to leave the United Kingdom far too soon. My professors at LSE, including Drs. Oscar Webber, Anna Cant, and Tanya Harmer, were inspiring teachers who encouraged me throughout the PhD applications process.

At Stanford, Professor Clayborne Carson introduced me to the foundational figures and texts within the Black radical tradition. His courses on African American history and social movements in the United States inspired generations of students to lead new movements and write new histories. Professor Richard White broadened my understanding of the nineteenth century in the United States. His lectures were so fascinating that I began to see the power and potential of history as a field. I will always cherish my memories of these classes.

The archivists, librarians, and historians in Pennsylvania, Alabama, Louisiana, New York, Bristol, and London, and everywhere in between, keep these stories documented and preserved. Thank you for your help in this project, including: Wendy Chmielewski at the Swarthmore College Peace Collection; John Tofanelli at the Columbia University Libraries; Cheryl Beredo at the Schomburg Center for Research in Black Culture; Philip Cunningham at the Amistad Research Center at Tulane University in New Orleans; Timothy Vasser, Jason Trawick, Derryn Moten, and Howard Robinson at the Alabama State University archives; Ken Barr at the Alabama Department of Archives and History; Samantha Boyle, Mark Small, and Dan Jones at the Bristol Archives; Anya Edmond at the Institute of Race Relations in London; and Mel Johnson and Karen Waddell at the British Library.

Randall Williams, Savannah Hollis, and the entire team at New-South Books made the daunting prospect of editing and publishing a book so much easier than I expected. They provided excellent guidance and suggestions throughout the creative process. Thank you to everyone at NewSouth for all you do.

My loved ones and friends, in New York, San Francisco, Stockholm, and London inspired me throughout the project and kept me as grounded as a graduate student can be. Isabelle Stromberg, thank you for your love and support and for putting up with my strange habit of running marathons every few months. The days spent gallivanting around Skansen are treasured memories. Kamakshi Duvvuru, while we no longer live in the same cramped co-op, I can always count on your friendship. I look forward to ambling around North Beach soon.

Finally, to my parents, John Manley and Kathy Sharp: I am so grateful for your love and support during all of my academic and personal journeys. Dad, you inspired my interest in reading and writing from a very young age, and you taught me so much more about the importance of love—something King, John Lewis, and the Montgomery Bus Boycott organizers understood so well. This project is dedicated to my parents, and to the memory and life of my father.

Introduction

'The Whole World Is Watching'

In late March 1956, Jo Ann Robinson addressed a mass meeting of hundreds of people at Holt Street Baptist Church in Montgomery, Alabama. As the three-month-old Montgomery Bus Boycott progressed, meetings rotated from one Black church to another. Black women constituted the majority of people sustaining the boycott, but few women had the opportunity to address such large gatherings. An English professor at Montgomery's Alabama State College (ASC), Robinson risked losing her teaching job by becoming a more visible leader, but she also understood that her address came at a pivotal moment during the boycott as a whole.

Robinson and others had already been the targets of white supremacist violence and intimidation. In February, a Montgomery police officer threw a stone through a window in Robinson's house, and, just two weeks later, another officer poured acid onto her car.[9] She continued to work sixteen-hour days, balancing her teaching duties alongside managing carpools, organizing Black Montgomery youth, and editing the Montgomery Improvement Association's (MIA) newsletter.[10]

Robinson realized that to maintain unity in the face of such violence, Black Montgomerians had to draw upon the deeper motivations behind their protest. Emphasizing the pride she felt

Jo Ann Robinson's arrest mug shot from February 1956 when she was among Montgomery leaders indicted for violating an anti-boycott law. (Courtesy Alabama State University)

to be Black in Montgomery, she referenced the international press coverage of the boycott to demonstrate its global significance. After acknowledging that her audience felt weary, she implored them to understand that "the whole world is watching the boycott . . . France, England, India are sending reporters here, because this is not a case, it is a social movement. The whole world respects us. I have never been so proud to be a Negro before." She then reiterated, "this is not a local movement. It has spread all over the United States. We can't get tired now."[11]

While the Montgomery Bus Boycott was undoubtedly grass-roots and local, Robinson understood that many in her audience were raised in Black churches, institutions with international ties, and inspired by a blend of Christian and transnational religious thinking. As Sarah Azaransky argues, African American Christian intellectuals and activists "believed that a Black social Christianity nourished by international and interreligious resources could fuel a movement for racial justice in the United States."[12] Proponents of an international Black Christianity, including theologians such as Benjamin Mays, and advocates of Gandhian nonviolence such as Pauli Murray and Bayard Rustin, trained and advised the young Montgomery minister, Martin Luther King Jr.[13]

King harmonized social gospel Christianity with Gandhian nonviolence, explaining after the boycott had concluded, "the spirit of passive resistance came to me from the Bible and the teachings of Jesus. The techniques of execution came from Gandhi."[14] King's understanding of Christianity was also shaped by spirituals that were rooted in the history of slavery in the United States.[15] Local, national, and transnational religious ideas circulated rapidly in Montgomery's Black churches, where theology was connected to the social and political realities facing Black people in the segregated South.

In Jim Crow Alabama, it was impossible for Black people to separate their politics from their lived realities. As the historian Robin Kelley argues, "for Southern Blacks in the age of Jim Crow, politics was not separate from lived experience or the imagined world of what is possible."[16] During their boycott, Black Montgomery organizers imagined many worlds. They imagined worlds where they could surely ride a bus to work without facing discrimination, but, more importantly, worlds where they could live out the full meaning and potential of justice and freedom.

King, Robinson, and others associated the boycott with larger movements for independence. The 1950s and 1960s represented the heyday of anticolonial wars of liberation, a period during which Black internationalism grew in power and influence. The boycott began just a few months after the 1955 Bandung Conference, where newly independent African and Asian states made commitments to global anticolonial solidarity.[17] Soon after the boycott concluded, King demonstrated his own solidarity with anticolonialism when he traveled to Ghana to celebrate its successful independence struggle, meeting the new Prime Minister Kwame Nkrumah.[18] Then, in 1959, King visited India to meet with comrades of Gandhi and heads of state including Prime Minister Jawaharlal Nehru.[19] While the Montgomery boycott began under a rather narrow rubric of improving conditions on buses, to varying degrees and at different intervals, Black Montgomery citizens understood that their protest resonated with freedom struggles around the world.

But how exactly did Black Montgomery organizers conceive of their boycott and its relationship to freedom struggles in other countries? How did a global pacifist organization, the Fellowship of Reconciliation (FOR), create an interpretation of the boycott that centered King as an actor? In responding to these questions, we consider another bus boycott in Bristol, England, in 1963, during which West Indians protested the city bus company's policy of refusing to hire Black bus drivers and conductors.

I argue that the Montgomery boycott was both a local and a global struggle due to two main factors. First, Montgomery organizers and FOR advisors connected their boycott to independence movements overseas. FOR activists contributed to popular associations of King with Gandhi by publishing an internationally distributed comic book read by anti-apartheid activists in South Africa. This comic book obscured the roles of Black women, but at the same time it highlighted the global connections between King and Gandhi.

Second, the Montgomery boycott became a global media event, stimulating coverage from international newspapers as well as independent accounts from the pacifist Left and Black internationalist groups. The transnational Black press, especially Claudia Jones in London, viewed the Montgomery and Bristol boycotts as part of a common struggle against racial injustice, despite tactical differences between the two movements. The Montgomery boycott was transnational in part because of how it was perceived and understood by activists in other countries and in other struggles, notably in the case of Paul Stephenson in Bristol. This was a process of historical adaptation through which new links were forged across the Black Atlantic. For Black internationalists, Montgomery became a useful reference point in movements ranging from the anti-apartheid struggle to the anti-color bar battles in the United Kingdom. The Montgomery boycott must thus be understood as part of the Black internationalist tradition and as part of the post–World War II era of independence struggles. The boycott has too often been considered only within the geographical and geopolitical confines of the United States South. This project seeks to highlight the boycott's global inspirations along with its local character.

The Montgomery Boycott in Scholarship

This book does not reiterate a timeline of actions in Montgomery, as a wave of scholarship in the 1980s led by David Garrow chronicled in meticulous detail the events of the Montgomery Bus Boycott and the rise of the Southern Christian Leadership Conference (SCLC).[20] Many secondary sources contextualize the civil rights movement alongside the federal government, highlighting President John F. Kennedy's (post-boycott) communications with King, and, later, President Lyndon B. Johnson's support for civil rights legislation.[21] The traditional history of the civil rights movement taught in many schools also generally begins with the Montgomery boycott in 1955 and concludes with the 1965 Voting Rights Act, a demarcation that simultaneously obscures grassroots activism, ignores interwar and

World War II-era organizing, divorces Black Power from preceding struggles, and, perhaps most dangerously, implies a linear trajectory of national progress towards the "promised land" of racial justice.

By contrast, this book explores the critical organizing by the Women's Political Council (WPC) during the late 1940s and early 1950s and links this work to the transnational ramifications of the Montgomery boycott. The transnational turn has mainly interrogated "the global" in major cities, however smaller southern United States cities were also centers of transnational struggle, community, and correspondence. Emphasizing the local and global qualities of protest challenges scholarship that de-emphasizes the radical imaginations of African American activists.[22]

Along with considering how anticommunism affected the Montgomery boycott, I draw on two major currents of scholarship: gender politics in Montgomery, and the Black Atlantic.[23] For some time, scholarship largely ignored the role of Black women in the Montgomery movement. By contrast, Jo Ann Robinson's 1987 memoir, *The Montgomery Bus Boycott and the Women Who Started It,* detailed the critical role of the WPC.[24] Memoirs from boycott participants, including Rosa Parks and Virginia Durr, have importantly redirected scholarly attention towards women in the WPC and the local NAACP branch.[25]

Work on the Black Atlantic informs how this dissertation connects Montgomery to racial justice struggles across the Atlantic. Kennetta Hammond Perry's *London Is the Place for Me* and Marc Matera's *Black London* address interwar and post-war organizing and migration by African Americans and Afro-Caribbeans.[26] Earl Lewis's call for African Americans to be written into a world of "overlapping diasporas" remains highly relevant for histories rooted in the U.S. South.[27] Through its contextualization within transnational organizing currents, the Montgomery struggle can be read as part of the Black Atlantic scholarly tradition.

The book proceeds along two paths. In Part I, "Gandhi, Montgomery, and the FOR Comic Book," I analyze how Gandhian nonviolence permeated various levels of the Montgomery boycott. While acknowledging the familial sources of King's transnational ideology, I focus on several key organizers and their awareness of Gandhian nonviolence and decolonization: Rosa Parks, Jo Ann Robinson, and Dr. Lawrence Reddick. Moving beyond Montgomery, I emphasize the role that the FOR played in the mythology of King as America's Gandhi, in some ways flattening King's political philosophy, while in other ways highlighting his global vision. Through a FOR comic book, the Montgomery boycott became known to activist circles in the United Kingdom and South Africa as King's struggle, rather than as a grassroots undertaking, and King was presented as a Gandhian peace prophet.

In Part II, "Montgomery and Bristol's Transnational Ties," I analyze the Bristol bus boycott of 1963 as a case study in envisaging how people in other countries interpreted the Montgomery boycott. I explore how protest in Alabama generated press coverage in Britain, inspired solidarity from British organizers and politicians, and contributed towards the successful resolution of the Bristol boycott.

My conclusion references the fracturing of racial justice movements during the late 1960s in the United Kingdom and the United States. I contend that scholarship needs to link the rise of Black Power in both countries to the transnational organizing of the more "conventional" phase of civil rights activism during the postwar years. Revisiting the Montgomery and Bristol boycotts can help modern-day participants in social movements understand how freedom struggles connect and relate to each other during a political moment when more Americans are becoming involved in protest movements than ever before.

THE UNLIKELY WORLD OF THE MONTGOMERY BUS BOYCOTT

I

Gandhi, Montgomery, and the FOR Comic Book

The Montgomery Bus Boycott became a local and global protest through organizing decisions made by Black people. Thus a review of the first few months of the boycott and organizers' strategic choices allows a deeper understanding of Montgomery's social and political environment. Assessing the historical significance of the Montgomery boycott requires understanding what made this movement so powerful and so united.

The Black people carrying out the boycott faced violence—the stakes of the struggle. It is sometimes too easy for observers of the boycott to gloss over the physical danger to the boycotters, violence that came in the form of daily police brutality, bombings, physical assaults and attacks, and random arrests and jailings. It can be difficult for the historian of the boycott to convey a sense of these dangers. Similarly, it can be difficult to express the extraordinary courage of those men, women, and children who risked their lives in a struggle for freedom. The 382-day long Montgomery boycott began as a protest with a rather narrow set of goals. On December 8, 1955, a week after Rosa Parks's protest, Martin Luther King Jr. and leaders of the Montgomery Improvement Association (MIA), the newly formed organization guiding the protest, met with White city and bus company officials. That meeting significantly shaped the stakes and trajectory of the struggle. The MIA proposed three modest demands: the first, "courteous treatment" on buses; the second, a first-come, first-served seating policy that would have maintained a system of Black riders having to sit rear to front on the bus and White riders front to rear; and, the third, the hiring of Black bus drivers on bus lines serving predominantly Black neighborhoods.[28] Officials rejected the demands. Later that same day, an MIA mass meeting at St. John's AME Church approved a carpool system that would be relied upon by thousands of Black people traveling within the city. This mass meeting, the second in the MIA's short existence, signaled to boycotters and to White officials that Black people were prepared to stay off the buses indefinitely.

As the movement progressed, Black Montgomery citizens understood that their protest had gained new imperatives. By its end, more than a year later, many understood that the boycott had become part of a struggle for freedom and justice, and that with each day Black people walked and car-pooled they were creating a new city and fashioning a new world. The level of local Black cooperation with the boycott was nearly universal. The Fisk University anthropologist Inez Adams traveled to Montgomery shortly after the boycott began, and in January 1956 she conducted a "census" of how many Black people were riding the buses. On January 24, she reported that during a one-hour period she saw just one Black bus rider. On another "cold, rainy day," out of 127 buses, she saw only 17 Black riders.[29] Potential Black bus riders were walking, but for those unable to walk, or for those who had much longer distances to traverse, the carpool system was a vital component in the long-term success of the boycott.

Effective social movements build solidarity, and this was

abundantly clear when Black men and women banded together in creating and maintaining the impromptu carpool system, one of the MIA's most creative actions. Cars were inaccessible to many working-class Blacks due to their cost, so many middle-class Blacks essentially donated their cars to the movement, either driving for hours each day picking up people, or loaning their cars to other drivers.

By all accounts, the carpool system built cross-class solidarity and inspired more people to dedicate their time and money to the movement. It was a genius stroke of organizing. Rufus Lewis—a member of King's Dexter Avenue Baptist Church, a colleague of Jo Ann Robinson at Alabama State College, and a voting rights activist for many years before the boycott—co-chaired the MIA's Transportation Committee. The system relied upon donations of tens, and eventually hundreds, of private cars, which had to be carefully maintained, fueled, and refueled. For those without gas money, the MIA fronted the cost. One of the most important components of the system was its intricate network of dispatch and pick-up stations, locations where people would congregate while awaiting rides.

Interviewed in January 1956 as the boycott progressed, Lewis explained that most dispatch centers were churches and voters' clubs: Black-owned institutions which provided the space and freedom necessary to maintain the carpools.[30] The fact that voters' clubs became central to the success of the dispatch system hints at the broader historical significance of Black voting mobilization in Montgomery. Throughout the 1940s and 1950s, E. D. Nixon, Jo Ann Robinson, Mary Fair Burks, and many other Black men and women fought the many restrictions and barriers facing Black voters in the segregated South. In attempting to register Black voters, these individuals faced violent resistance from a political system that attempted to maintain white supremacy by limiting Black political participation. The tradition of White suppression of Black voting had a long history in Montgomery and the United States. Since Reconstruction following the Civil War, which saw Black politicians elected to Congress, white supremacist groups such as the Ku Klux Klan mobilized to roll back the expansion of democracy and political expression. Black organizers knew that their right to vote challenged an edifice of white supremacy, and they knew how white supremacists would react. Voters' clubs played an under-recognized role in the maintenance of the carpool system, and these institutions reflected this longer history of voting activism. Without Black churches or the voting organizations that had been active in Montgomery for decades, Black people would have risked boarding and exiting the carpools at White-owned properties, meaning that they would have been easier targets for white-supremacist violence and retaliation by vigilantes and police. The network of pickup and dispatch locations was extensive. In late December or early January there were twenty pickup stations, and by the end of January, thirty-five or forty. Dispatch stations swelled during the same period from thirty to forty-five.[31]

The backbone of the carpool system was its many hundreds of drivers. These Black men and women kept driving even as they were followed by Montgomery police and arrested at random. A driver recalled in January 1956 that one day he drove forty-nine people to work. He kept his car in the pool from 6 a.m. to 10 p.m. every day.[32] These were not unusual statistics for the dedicated carpool drivers who kept the boycott moving.

Small numbers of Whites also participated in the carpools. Virginia Durr was one of the few White women to publicly support the boycott, along with her husband, Clifford. She recalled the power of watching elderly Black women walking through the city, explaining in a March 1956 letter, "some of the old women almost have to creep along . . . and I pick up all the ones I can, and as they never know whether you are a friend or foe, they always refuse to say anything about why they are not riding the bus."[33] The letter illustrated some of the complicated racial politics in Montgomery during the boycott. Given the bombings of Black homes and churches, and the constant threat of police violence and harassment, some Blacks were wary of Whites who expressed support. The presence of police spies, who attempted to infiltrate the MIA and who recorded some of its mass meetings, also made Blacks cautious.

Although Virginia Durr grew up in a conservative and wealthy Alabama family, she recognized her position as an important ally to the movement. During the 1930s and 1940s, the Durrs lived in Washington, D.C., and became part of a circle of White Southern New Dealers. He was a government lawyer, and she joined the Southern Conference for Human Welfare (SCHW), an interracial organization combatting segregation. Later she campaigned for a Virginia Senate seat as a Progressive Party candidate with an anti-war platform.[34] By the time the Durrs returned to Montgomery in 1951, she was an outspoken and experienced political organizer and commentator.

While she maintained friendships with Rosa Parks and other Black organizers, Durr recognized that she was still an outsider to the movement due to her racial and class privilege and due to the politics of racial segregation in Montgomery. She understood that the boycott had to be led by Blacks, writing that "this started with the Negroes, it is run by them . . . and while our help can be offered . . . they are bearing the burden."[35] Supporting the carpool was Durr's way of assisting the boycott by using her privilege. As a White woman, Durr understood that if she was questioned by police about why she was driving Black people through the city, she could explain the situation by saying that the passengers were domestic workers. Gender politics in Montgomery, while confining women to domestic roles and limiting job opportunities, also created narrow political possibilities for any upper-class women sympathetic to the boycott. Some White upper-class women ignored the fact that domestic workers participated in the boycott because they did not want to lose the labor of Black women.

Other White women did not believe that their domestic workers would participate. In 1974, Durr recalled that "the dependence, you see, of the women on the Black maids was so great that they just had no idea . . . there were fleets of cars going back and forth from Black and White neighborhoods every day, taking the maids back and forth."[36] This reliance on Black labor exposed the everyday hypocrisies of segregation in Montgomery, a system which did not allow Blacks in the front of buses, but which depended on Blacks for the functioning of the city. When buses no longer transported Black women to the homes of upper-class White women, some White women responded by picking up domestic workers themselves, thus facilitating the boycott.

Meanwhile, Montgomery authorities contorted themselves legally trying to disband the carpool, so threatened were they by its effectiveness. In late February 1956, city officials indicted eighty-nine boycott leaders, including King, for violating an obscure state anti-boycott law from 1921. The law, which prohibited "conspiracies that interfered with lawful business," had been implemented in response to an interracial coal mining strike in Birmingham in 1920.[37] The strike, one of many protests by coal miners, hinted at the promises and challenges of interracial unionism in Alabama.[38] While the effort to secure better working conditions and wages was unsuccessful, the threat to Alabama's mining oligarchs was serious enough to merit new legislation restricting cross-racial organizing and strikes.

Despite the obvious differences between the 1920 strike and the 1955–56 boycott, Montgomery authorities relied on this legislation in indicting the movement. On March 1, Lewis reported to a mass meeting at Holt Street Baptist Church that the mass arrests had "deteriorated" the transportation system. He implored his audience that "we need you now more than ever. Register your cars in the pools. We need more cars . . . now. The spirit of the group is what has kept the transportation going."[39] The pleas for unity worked, and the carpool system continued with renewed commitment.

The mass arrests did not cow the boycott into acquiescence, but instead triggered sympathetic national and international media attention.[40] The story made the front page of the *New York Times*, which until this point had shown little interest in the movement.[41] By late February 1956, Japanese, French, and British newspapers stationed reporters in Montgomery to cover the story, another sign of the boycott's global relevance and importance.[42]

DANGER IN STRUGGLE

Despite the growing media focus on Montgomery, the boycott was not destined to win. The success of the movement depended on the ongoing unity of Black people, a level of solidarity that demonstrated enormous courage given the immediate stakes and danger of the boycott. Supporting the Montgomery movement meant risking one's life and safety and that of one's family. This was abundantly clear just weeks into the boycott when in late January 1956 white supremacists bombed Martin Luther King Jr.'s home with his wife, Coretta Scott King, and their infant daughter inside.[43] Luckily, no one was injured in the attack. Addressing the crowd of agitated Blacks who gathered outside his home, Dr. King appealed for the peaceful continuation of the boycott.

Often, violence towards Blacks was carried out by local police and vigilantes acting in concert, a reminder of the danger of the day's political moment. Before Birmingham, Alabama, became known as "Bombingham," the same could have been said about Montgomery. Though today the Montgomery boycott is held up as an acceptable form of protest, at the time, movement participants risked their lives each time they walked or carpooled to work and each time they gathered for mass meetings.

A few White Montgomery residents publicly supported the boycott and noted its parallels to Gandhian nonviolence. Several weeks before King began publicly linking the boycott to Gandhi, the librarian Juliette Morgan identified connections between the struggle in Montgomery and Gandhian nonviolence.[44] A week after the Montgomery boycott began, Morgan appealed to the major city newspaper, the *Montgomery Advertiser*. In "Lesson From Gandhi," she wrote, "the spirit animating our Negro citizens as they ride these taxis or walk from the heart of Cloverdale to Mobile Road has been . . . like that of Gandhi."[45]

Jeannie and Robert Graetz would have agreed with Morgan's editorial. The Graetzes were newcomers to Montgomery, having moved to Alabama just a few months before the boycott, and Robert Graetz was the minister of an all-Black congregation.[46] The Graetzes' Whiteness did not protect them from attacks, and white supremacists bombed the Graetzes home, as well.[47]

In December 1955, many readers of the *Advertiser* viewed the boycott as a breakdown of law and order, not an example of Gandhian protest. A December 22, 1955, letter to the *Advertiser* summarized the view of many in arguing that Black people were "encouraging their race to disregard law and order."[48] Tragically, Morgan ultimately lost her life because of the anxiety she faced. On a regular basis, she answered phone calls from people threatening to kill her. Fired from her job and deeply depressed by hostility, she committed suicide in the summer of 1957.[49]

AMERICA'S GANDHI

As the boycott continued and King's name became better known, increasing numbers of observers drew parallels with Gandhi. Glenn Smiley helped popularize the notion that King could be "America's Gandhi." Smiley traveled to Montgomery as a representative of the Fellowship of Reconciliation (FOR), the pacifist organization which had started in the United Kingdom after World War I and had grown to include branches across the United States. Led by the minister A. J. Muste, the FOR played a major role in supporting the boycott through advisors, including Smiley and Bayard Rustin, and through financial donations to the Montgomery Improvement Association.

In a February 24, 1956, letter to King, Charles Lawrence, the national chair of FOR, explained, "while our organization is very anxious to 'do something,' we do not wish to do anything which your group would feel unwise or ill-timed. You are doing too good a job to have it unwittingly harmed by even the best-meaning groups."[50]

Aware of its outsider status, with offices in New York and largely Northern and White membership, FOR nonetheless was composed of experienced activists who believed they could guide the MIA. Compared to the NAACP, which at times felt threatened by the MIA's media coverage and sometimes disagreed with the direct-action tactics of the boycott, the FOR supported nonviolent civil disobedience.

When Smiley arrived in Montgomery in late February 1956 and met with King, he was struck by the young minister's leadership ability, eloquence, and determination. Smiley wrote to FOR colleagues and said that he "just had one of the most glorious, yet tragic interviews I have ever had," describing him as possibly a "Negro Gandhi, or he can be made into an unfortunate [demagogue] destined to swing from a lynch mob's tree."[51] Smiley sensed that "if he can *really* be won to a faith in nonviolence there is no end to what he can do."[52] While there is an obvious paternalism in Smiley's correspondence, he was correct that the Montgomery movement was at a critical turning point. It was still unclear how the boycott would respond to the bombings of movement leaders, to the attacks on Jo Ann Robinson and others, and to police coercion.

The veteran organizer Bayard Rustin had arrived in Montgomery a few days before Smiley. By 1956, Rustin had been excommunicated from the FOR because of an arrest for homosexual activity in 1953.[53] Anti-communism during the 1950s narrowed acceptable standards for gender and sexuality, revealing homophobia in even the most radical civil rights and pacifist organizations. Upon meeting with King, Rustin had a similar reaction as his colleague. He realized that King was "developing a decidedly Gandhi-like view and recognizes that there is a tremendous educational job to be done within the Negro community."[54] At the same time, when Rustin noticed guns in King's house and bodyguards surrounding it, he sensed that the boycott could turn violent.[55] Smiley and Rustin saw King as the key individual who could help translate Gandhian knowledge to the masses.

But others within the MIA had far greater experience than King in studying and participating in nonviolent social movements. Remembered for staying in her bus seat on December 1, 1955, the protest which ignited the boycott, Rosa Parks was a veteran organizer in Alabama who, throughout the 1940s, attended NAACP meetings and state conventions. The historian Jeannie Theoharis notes that "Parks made the decision to remain in her seat through her own political will and long history of bus resistance."[56]

Just months before the boycott, at the Highlander Folk School in Tennessee, Parks met with practitioners of nonviolent resistance during a two-week conference. In her memoir, she recalled how liberating it was to live in an environment free of segregation, remembering, "one of my greatest pleasures there was enjoying the smell of bacon frying and coffee brewing and knowing that the White folks were doing the preparing instead of me."[57] Attending workshops on school desegregation, Parks and other participants were "encouraged to contextualize the problems facing their communities within a global movement for human rights and to come up with concrete steps to create change locally."[58]

The Highlander pedagogy embraced a local and grassroots approach to organizing while at the same time emphasizing a global vision for change, a pedagogy facilitated by its many international visitors. By the time Parks visited in 1955, Highlander was a stopping point for Gandhian activists touring the United States. In 1951, the socialist organizer and Gandhian Ram Manohar Lohia visited Highlander and met its founder, Myles Horton. During his visit, Lohia revisited Gandhian struggle, explaining, "Gandhi invited us to get the British out by our own suffering, by refusing to obey them and going to jail."[59] In attending the Highlander conference, Parks participated in a well-established forum for knowledge-sharing between the Black struggle for freedom and the Indian independence movement. She described her December 1 arrest by recalling the protest in terms that paralleled Gandhian thinking: "'If I did not resist being mistreated, then I would spend the rest of my life being mistreated.'"[60] Parks's visit to Highlander strengthened her convictions about nonviolent resistance and illuminated the connections between freedom struggles around the world.

A Christian Gandhi?

Why did peace activists look towards King as the link to Gandhian nonviolence, and not Parks?[61] Civil rights and peace organizations simply did not view Black women as leaders of the boycott, and their international correspondence thus privileged King. John Nevin Sayre popularized the Gandhi-King connection internationally, especially to FOR activists in the United Kingdom. The chair of the International FOR, Sayre was an American peace movement leader who was well-connected to Gandhian circles in Europe and around the world.[62] In April 1956, Sayre wrote to one of his FOR colleagues in London, Vera Brittain. Sayre told Brittain about the "nonviolent bus strike in Montgomery, Alabama," adding, "Martin Luther King Jr., the young Negro pastor who has emerged as a Christian Gandhi, is only twenty-seven years old. The older man who really started this bus strike was one of the most respected of Montgomery's Negro citizens."[63]

Sayre's letter ignored the role of women in organizing the boycott, instead concluding that the veteran Montgomery organizer E. D. Nixon was responsible for the protest. Nixon did play an important role in the boycott, advising Jo Ann Robinson and many others, but Sayre did not mention Parks or Robinson. His description of King as a "Christian Gandhi" did advertise King as a transnational religious figure. He emphasized King's ideological similarities with FOR, implicitly suggesting that the minister could become the peace prophet that FOR was looking to send on world tours.

In the 1930s, the FOR sent traveling secretaries to spread the pacifist message to Latin America, Africa, and Asia.[64] Muriel Lester traveled the world on behalf of FOR, popularizing the gospel of Christian pacifism and Gandhian nonviolence. In 1926, she visited India and stayed at Gandhi's ashram for a month.[65] Following World

War II, and with Cold War tensions rising, Sayre probably conceived of King as someone who could carry on Lester's role. In June 1956, Sayre wrote to Lester updating her about the "Montgomery bus strike," explaining, "it's Gandhi coming to life in the U.S.A. and the FOR has been assisting at the Resurrection."[66]

While Sayre updated British FOR activists about the "Christian Gandhi" emerging in Montgomery, American disciples of Gandhi wrote to King around the same time expressing their solidarity. Like Lester, many of these people had traveled to India to learn about Gandhian nonviolence. On March 21, William Stuart Nelson wrote to King to express his support for the boycott. The dean of Howard University, Nelson marched with Gandhi in 1946 as part of the American Friends Service Committee (AFSC), and he told King, "Once I asked [Gandhi] . . . whether his method of nonviolent noncooperation might prove successful in the struggle here for our rights. Now it appears that you are experimenting in that direction."[67]

Importantly, many of King's Gandhian correspondents stressed the anticolonial implications of Gandhi's life as much as his teachings on nonviolence.[68] Pacifists within and without the FOR believed in an active form of nonviolent resistance linked to anticolonial struggle, and they saw in King someone who could carry Gandhi's torch as the next prophet of peace and justice.

King's public statements increasingly reflected the influence of his Gandhian correspondents. Addressing an interracial audience in Brooklyn in late March 1956, King said "'Christ showed us the way, and Gandhi in India showed it could work.'"[69] He added that Gandhi used nonviolence "'to break loose from the political and economical domination by the British and brought the British Empire to its knees. Let's now use this method in the United States.'"[70] References to the British Empire showcased how King

41

saw similarities between anticolonial struggles and racial justice movements in the United States.

King's embrace of Gandhi was rooted in the Black anticolonial tradition and in Black liberation theology, a theology defined by James Cone which draws on the social gospel teachings of the Bible. Cone argues that Black liberation theology "arises from an identification with the oppressed Blacks of America, seeking to interpret the gospel of Christ in the light of the Black condition."[71] King's support for liberation theology was itself a reaction against liberal theology. As a young theological student, King critiqued liberal theology in a school essay as becoming "so involved in higher criticism [that it] . . . seems to be too divorced from life."[72] Black liberation theology was the antidote to religious training that King sometimes found disconnected from the racial and economic injustice facing Black people in the United States.

The historian Nico Slate argues that "King's Gandhi . . . much more than a symbol of nonviolence, embodied the power of colored cosmopolitanism wedded to the liberation theology of the Black church."[73] King understood that Gandhian philosophy involved far more than tactical discussions about nonviolence and violence. Gandhian nonviolence informed anticolonial movements then unfolding across Africa and Asia.

Anticolonialism and liberation theology inspired King's global thinking and encouraged him to align his public addresses on the boycott with independence movements overseas. In March 1956, while preaching to the MIA, he proclaimed "solidarity with independence movements in Asia and Africa," explaining, "we are God's children . . . tired of being suppressed politically [and] economically; tired of being segregated and discriminated."[74]

Like Gandhi, King recognized that social movements could transform struggles in faraway places. In his sermons and speeches,

King often referenced an interconnected and interdependent world, explaining that out of this "world house" there could emerge a "beloved community."[75] When King embraced Gandhian ideology and supported decolonization movements, he expressed his global awareness, a perspective that stemmed from his upbringing in the borderless Black Baptist church. His father, grandfather, and great-grandfather were all Baptist ministers.[76]

Born in Atlanta, Georgia, on the eve of the Great Depression, King witnessed the great poverty facing White and Black people. In an "Autobiography of Religious Development," he remembered asking his parents about breadlines around the city, adding, "I can see the effects of this early childhood experience on my present anti-capitalistic feelings."[77] The future minister was from a young age introspective, and he recalled, "it is quite easy for me to think of a God of love mainly because I grew up in a family where love was central."[78]

Through their love, King's family instilled in him a strong belief in human potential. *From Civil Rights to Human Rights* remains one of the foundational texts concerning King's personal development, and Thomas Jackson argues that "King Jr. inherited a determination to fight economic and racial injustice from his family and community."[79] The Black social gospel tradition was the primary source material for many of these lessons.

When King decided on a career in the ministry and attended Crozer Theological Seminary in Pennsylvania, he learned, from theologians dedicated to the social gospel, a theology tied to economic and political realities that calls for reforming society as well as individuals. Jackson argues that "King's liberal and progressive instructors nurtured his sense of a loving, suffering, personal God . . . manifest in human service."[80] In class assignments, King "addressed the political and economic sins of militarism, poverty, and slavery."[81] His global thinking during the Montgomery boycott was in many ways an unsurprising outcome given his familial and theological education. As King understood it, the social gospel was a borderless and transnational concept that could be adapted to interpret political events ranging from the Montgomery boycott to anticolonial wars of liberation. The social gospel reaffirmed King's belief in a redemptive kind of Christianity and provided a system of moral and political values that he drew upon during his leadership of the Montgomery boycott.

Jo Ann Robinson and Many Thousands of Leaders

While King developed his personal liberation theology, Robinson dedicated herself to the unpaid and largely unrecognized civil rights organizing that took place years before the boycott, labor led by Black women. Born in Georgia, Robinson was the valedictorian of her high school and the first in her family to graduate from college. After receiving a master's in English at Atlanta University, she joined the faculty at Alabama State College and, like other colleagues, attended services at King's future congregation, Dexter Avenue Baptist Church.[82]

Long before her work in the MIA, Robinson participated in the Women's Political Council. ASC Professor Mary Fair Burks founded the Montgomery organization in 1946, and Robinson joined in 1949, becoming president a year later.[83] Although most scholarship did not recognize its importance—J. Mills Thornton III's 1980 article was a rare exception—the WPC became one of the most active and militant Black civic organizations in Montgomery.[84] Made up of mostly middle-class Black women, the WPC organized voting drives and petitioned local government for reforms, mobilizing Blacks to stand up for their civil rights. In December 1955, the WPC publicized the Montgomery boycott by distributing perhaps fifty thousand leaflets around the city.[85] Robinson wrote and helped to mimeograph the leaflet, which stated to Black people plainly, "Don't ride the bus to work, to town, to school, or any place Monday, December 5. Another Negro Woman has been arrested and put in jail because she refused to give up her bus seat."[86] Without such mass dissemination, it is unlikely that the boycott would have received the almost universal support that it did.

When Robinson learned about Parks's arrest, she saw a glorious opportunity for direct action. For several years, Robinson and E. D. Nixon, a leading union organizer and NAACP activist in Montgomery, had discussed a possible bus boycott. Similar to Rosa Parks, in 1949 Robinson had been forced off a Montgomery bus for sitting in the White section.[87] The trauma of that bus ride focused her attention towards city government and the Montgomery City Lines, the company that operated the buses under a city franchise.[88] During the early 1950s, Robinson, Nixon, Rufus Lewis, and members of the WPC petitioned city commissioners, and in 1954 she wrote a letter on behalf of the WPC to Montgomery Mayor W. A. Gayle. In the letter, she threatened Gayle with a boycott of the buses unless changes were made. The document illustrated that for some time Black women had made their grievances about treatment on the buses clear to White politicians, who ignored and downplayed their concerns.[89]

Rather than remember Robinson's organizing as unprecedented, we should consider the rich tradition of organizing among Black women in the South who resisted segregation on buses and streetcars. While Montgomery became the prototypical bus boycott, other boycotts, of varying degrees of formality and involving various numbers of participants, occurred throughout the South before and after 1955. Robin Kelley highlights this history by focusing on protests in Birmingham in the early twentieth century.[90] Kelley argues that the bus was an ideal place for protest because it became a kind of "moving theater," a space where segregation was laid bare for all to see. The bus and the streetcar were confined spaces where harassment by White bus drivers and the daily injustices of segregation could be confronted and exposed for White and Black bus riders. While records are incomplete, Kelley asserts that Black women "outnumbered" Black men in "incidents of resistance on buses and streetcars."[91]

In part, Black women rode public transit more than most Black men because many of the former were domestic workers who had to travel across segregated Southern cities to get to wealthier White neighborhoods. But there was also a long protest tradition that Robinson and Parks joined when they confronted segregation on Montgomery buses. Black women including Sojourner Truth and Ida B. Wells-Barnett had also personally confronted and opposed Jim Crow on public transit.[92] In the realm of buses and streetcars, Robinson's organizing and Parks's protest were part of a much longer history of protest. Given that both women were experienced organizers, they were probably intimately familiar with this history.

Montgomery organizers recognized that the December 1955 boycott was hardly a new idea and that the WPC had mobilized Black people to consider drastic action before. In a January 20, 1956, interview, Rufus Lewis, the co-chair of the Transportation Committee of the MIA, explained, "Mrs. Robinson . . . has been the main advocate for boycotting the bus for the last two or three years."[93] Donald Ferron interviewed Lewis as the boycott unfolded, and in his "interviewer's note" Ferron added, "the public recognizes Reverend King as the leader, but I wonder if Mrs. Robinson may be of equal importance."[94] When Parks was arrested, Robinson, Burks, and the WPC guided the movement during its infancy. Robinson recalled in a 1984 interview that "there had been so many things that happened, that the Black women had been embarrassed over, and they were ready to explode."[95]

Throughout the boycott, Robinson drew upon diverse sources of inspiration as the editor of the MIA newsletter. In her September 1956 edition, which reached tens of thousands of Black people, she connected Montgomery to Gandhian independence.[96] She wrote that "the underlying philosophy of the Montgomery movement is . . . passive resistance . . . Through this method Gandhi was able to free India from British domination. It has freed the hearts and minds of Negro Montgomerians, who [are] learning for the first time the real meaning of love."[97] As Robinson had demonstrated in her March 1956 address, in which she explained that the entire world was watching the boycott, she had long understood how the Montgomery protest had become a campaign with global reach and influence.

It is difficult to determine causality when explaining how Gandhian ideology influenced the Montgomery struggle and overly simplistic to say that Robinson and other boycott participants were directly inspired by Gandhi. Certainly, participants stayed off the buses for different reasons. For many who had lived under segregation their entire lives, treatment on Montgomery buses could no longer be tolerated and had to be confronted en masse. What is clear from analyzing Robinson's address and newsletter is that Gandhian nonviolence was an important historical reference point during the Montgomery movement. When she related Montgomery to Indian independence, she connected a struggle against segregation to anticolonialism, inspiring her audiences to think about the boycott through the lens of global solidarity. Nonviolence was the relational tie bridging movements many thousands of miles apart.

Robinson was probably careful to espouse predominantly non-violent anticolonial struggles and not more violent struggles such as the war in Algeria, which had ignited in 1954. She was aware that any violence on the part of Montgomery Blacks would have been met with intense counterattacks from White police and vigilantes, and that a turn to violent tactics could have discredited the movement as a whole. For Robinson, nonviolence was not simply a political or rhetorical choice but also a powerful tool because of what it could affect in the "hearts and minds" of Black people in Montgomery.[98] She alluded to the power of love, what King would term the power of "agape," a "spontaneous" and "creative" kind of love unmotivated by selfish pursuits.[99] This was a love rooted in struggle and in sacrifice. In the spring of 1956, unlike King, she was not invited to speak at universities and churches, was not interviewed by national media outlets, and had far fewer opportunities to expound upon her philosophical convictions. Nonetheless, scholarship ignored for too long her global vision and her anticolonial solidarity.

Robinson taught at one of the few Montgomery institutions, Alabama State College, which did not, at least initially, curtail her organizing. Founded in 1867 by freed slaves, the historically Black college provided not just education and career advancement for Black Montgomery students and teachers but also community and political mobilization.[100] The departments of English and History were oases within the sea of segregation where an educated Black middle class built new political alliances as the boycott unfolded. Along with Burks and Robinson, Dr. Lawrence Reddick, chair of the history department, participated in the boycott.[101] As a historian writing about the boycott, Reddick was in a unique position to interpret its significance during the era of decolonization.

In an address in February 1956, he reiterated Robinson's point that "the eyes of the world are on Montgomery," adding that the medium-sized city was "a classic struggle for democracy and human dignity."[102] To him, the boycott was not merely about desegregating Montgomery buses; it had become a "struggle for democracy" that would alter America's relationship to newly independent African and Asian countries. During the Bandung Conference period of burgeoning anticolonial solidarity, Reddick recognized that newly independent countries were looking critically towards the United States' domestic politics.

These Asian and African countries sought to build democratic systems of governance in a post-colonial world, and the success or failure of the Montgomery boycott would confirm one of two geopolitical realities. If the boycott failed, the United States' racial inequalities would make it unsuitable as a model for political governance, driving nations away from the superpower. But if the boycott succeeded, newly independent countries would continue to learn from and align themselves with the promises of American democracy—at least that was what many liberals imagined. Reddick understood that the stakes of the Montgomery struggle were truly global and that the boycott would transform geopolitics and diplomacy depending on how the movement unfolded.

Reddick's and Robinson's perspectives were noteworthy due to their standings within the boycott, and other members of the MIA shared similar feelings about the boycott's ties to anticolonialism. On February 1, 1956, Prince Conley, an NAACP member also on the executive committee of the MIA, reflected upon the global influence of the boycott. He said that the boycott "seems to be a world movement with the darker people trying to rise up against colonialism," and added that "the people were just fed up."[103] For its leaders and for its rank and file, the boycott had become an example of global solidarity.

In February 1956 far away from Alabama, Americans reading about the boycott also realized the international stakes of the

Montgomery struggle, framing the movement alongside Cold War politics and decolonization. Alabama Governor James E. Folsom received hundreds of letters, not just from Alabama, from White segregationists as well as from liberals, who feared that Montgomery's racial oppression could trigger newly independent nations to turn towards the Soviet Union and embrace communism. A February 23 letter from Alice Cole of Tacoma, Washington, warned Folsom that "nothing that has happened in the U.S. could give more aid and comfort to our presumed enemy, the U.S.S.R. than the things that have happened recently in Alabama." Cole continued, "No communist nor group of communists could so effectively undermine our position in the world. We send our boys, including Negro boys, around the globe, to defend 'freedom' and the 'American way of life'——and then permit such conditions to exist in our own front yard that make our talk ridiculous."[104]

Four days later, Folsom received another letter from someone fearing political backlash. J. Welch from North Carolina reiterated that "the whole world is watching what is going on in Montgomery. Two-thirds of the world's population is colored and we need all the allies we can get. Such treatment as the negroes in Montgomery are receiving is driving India and other countries into the communist camp."[105] Seeing Governor Folsom as a key power broker in Alabama, these outsiders to the boycott realized what participants like Reddick had come to understand: the freedom struggle in Montgomery could influence the United States' standing in world politics and hinder or aid in the Cold War against the Soviet Union.

The FOR, meanwhile, recognized that the Montgomery boycott might aid nonviolent struggles around the world through more pragmatic and direct means, if only organizers had some text they could turn to for inspiration.

The Montgomery Story Overseas

During the first few months of the boycott, the FOR had played an important role in publicizing the Gandhi-King connection to peace activists. For the Montgomery boycott to become a global struggle as it did, however, took a convergence of events sparked by FOR publishing an internationally distributed comic book, *Martin Luther King and the Montgomery Story*. FOR's director of publications, Alfred Hassler, proposed the idea in November 1956.

Since the 1930s, comic books had been hugely popular in the United States,[106] yet they faced growing cultural backlash[107] as parents and politicians linked their popularity to juvenile delinquency, crime, and homosexuality.[108] These concerns resulted in the 1954 Comics Code, which eliminated much of the sex, violence, and graphic content of earlier titles.[109] The Cold War political climate also resulted in numerous titles depicting the dangers of communist infiltration in American society.[110] FOR would have been aware of this cultural stigma, but it also likely realized that the comic book genre allowed for ideas about nonviolence to reach more people and a younger audience.

A comic book centered on the Montgomery story also bucked decades-long industry trends regarding the politics of race. The most profitable comics generally depicted heroes as White and villains as people of color. Comic book historians have described this "comics pedagogy" as "White patriarchal universalism," the process by which "comics tell a story about White heroes and minority villains, White victors and minority losers, White protagonists and perhaps a minority sidekick."[111]

By the summer of 1957, the FOR comic book had acquired a clear subject: King. Apart from a reference to Rosa Parks, the comic book reified gender stereotypes within the industry and excluded women.[112] There is no mention of Joann Robinson and the pivotal

*Cover of the comic book that inspired readers worldwide.
© 1957 Fellowship of Reconciliation, www.forusa.org.
Reprinted by permission. All rights reserved.*

role of the WPC in publicizing the boycott. Some picked up on these erasures, with a member of the Mennonite Central Committee complaining to Hassler that there was "too much adulation" of King.[113] But the comic book was not designed to represent the diverse nature of the Montgomery struggle. It was intended to position King as a Gandhian hero. Sections highlighted the bombing of King's home, cross burnings, and attacks by the KKK.

After detailing the violence that boycotters faced and lauding King's nonviolent leadership, the FOR moved to its main objective: providing activists and organizers in other countries with a handbook on nonviolent resistance. Hassler explained that the comic book "would get across in human terms . . . the importance of dealing with the whole struggle in nonviolent, Christian, potentially reconciling terms rather than with violence and bitterness."[114] The last section of the book was entitled, "How the Montgomery Method Works," and it moved from narrative description to prescription, spelling out tactical choices activists could make during nonviolent struggles.

Direct and didactic, the comic book was designed to appeal to a broad audience of readers, many of whom, the FOR anticipated, would not be literate. In a 1997 letter, Richard Deats reflected upon the FOR's expectations. While Deats was not directly responsible for the comic book, he was a leader in the organization who had joined after listening to one of Muriel Lester's lectures.[115] Deats became the FOR's director of communications and led nonviolence workshops in South Africa and many other countries.[116] He wrote in 1997 that the comic book "was originally intended to convey to semiliterate persons the story of nonviolence and its effectiveness as seen in the Montgomery movement. The medium of the highly popular comic book was believed to be the best way to reach masses of exploited African Americans."[117] Certainly, it is hard to gauge from Deats's letter, written decades later, whether the FOR knew the literacy level of its audience and whether these estimations were accurate, but the letter is telling because of what it highlights about the FOR's intentions. By design, the FOR aimed to disseminate the comic book as widely as possible in the hope that the world would learn about the Montgomery story.

In contrast to newspaper articles from the time which usually only mentioned Gandhi's name in connection to King and Montgomery, the comic book delved into greater detail about the Indian independence movement. In a panel featuring an image of Gandhi, the comic book explained that "again and again they put Gandhi in prison, but that did not stop him," adding, "It became harder and harder for the British to keep control. Their jails were filled with India's best-loved leaders."[118] The FOR wanted readers of the comic book to fnote the similarities between the treatment of Indians by British colonial officials and the treatment of African Americans by Montgomery law enforcement.

The comic book also simplified and ignored various aspects of Gandhi's life, particularly his time in South Africa. Before he became an internationally known independence leader, Gandhi was a young lawyer living in the British colonies and republics that today make up South Africa. He spent more than two decades in the region, from the late nineteenth through the early twentieth century, a time of great political upheaval. As the First and Second Anglo-Boer Wars raged, eventually establishing the Union of South Africa in 1910, Gandhi became politicized by the colonial color bars and racial discrimination that Indian people faced. In his autobiography, Gandhi described leading the Natal Indian Congress and organizing strikes and boycotts in defiance of pass laws—legislation that restricted the movement of Indian people and anyone who was not White.[119] Yet his activism on behalf of Indians did not include solidarity with Black South Africans.

In linking King with Gandhi, the FOR sought to dramatize King as a pacifist leader who could inspire nonviolent resistance around the world. © 1957 Fellowship of Reconciliation, www.forusa.org. Reprinted by permission. All rights reserved.

He focused on the political challenges facing Indians, instead of considering how colonialism created and maintained racial hierarchies. Gandhi would often refer to Zulu people in southern Africa by using a racial pejorative, perhaps without considering its meaning.[120] Even among Indians, Gandhi expressed views which privileged the merchant class.[121] Scholars have pointed out Gandhi's racial and class bias during his years in South Africa.[122] These were biases which paralleled Gandhi's later ideas about caste in India, something his contemporary B. R. Ambedkar critiqued.

Over the course of Gandhi's life, his politics evolved, and he came to embrace ideas that he had overlooked earlier. During his time in South Africa, Gandhi had not yet developed the political ideology and lifestyle that he would term "satyagraha," meaning truth force, which became a system of values and practices that shaped his nonviolent struggle against British colonialism. Before satyagraha, Gandhi developed a politics that revolved around the racial discrimination facing Indians, a focus that stemmed from an incident on public transit.

In his memoir, he described the moment when he was thrown off a racially segregated train because he refused to sit in a lower-class section. The experience paralleled Rosa Parks's treatment on Montgomery buses and led to a political awakening.[123] The loneliness and sadness Gandhi felt after this confrontation with segregation triggered a desire to become more politically active, foreshadowing his work in the Natal Indian Congress.

The peace studies professor, writer, and activist Michael Nagler has suggested that Gandhi's life remains inspirational because of his personal transformation.[124] After his years as a relatively privileged and conservative lawyer, he became a creative and visionary independence leader. Gradually, he broadened his critique of colonialism to include Indians of different castes, including "untouchables," although these pivots happened later, upon his returning to India from South Africa. For the purposes of this project, it is less important to assess Gandhi's politics and more interesting to note how the FOR comic book overlooked, or perhaps intentionally ignored, his time in South Africa. This fact is ironic given how influential the comic book became when it was published and distributed in the country.

THE COMIC BOOK IN SOUTH AFRICA

While it is difficult to gauge how books are received, especially on an international scale, the comic book created a mythology of the Montgomery boycott that shaped perceptions of King and the United States civil rights movement. The comic book was published in December 1957 and quickly became FOR's most successful publishing event, with 200,000 to 250,000 copies sold and distributed around the world.[125]

The global distribution of the comic book is one way of tracing social movements across the Atlantic. In the United Kingdom, the international pacifist weekly *Peace News* serialized the comic book in as many as fourteen installments in which British readers learned each week about the next development in the Montgomery story.[126] By 1958, the comic book had reached South Africa, where determined anti-apartheid activists and religious leaders printed and copied the book to ever-widening circles of readers.[127] At some point that year, Brian Bunting saw the comic book in *Peace News*. A White anti-apartheid activist, Bunting was born in Johannesburg to parents who founded the South African Communist Party. After serving in World War II, Bunting edited six radical newspapers, each banned by the Afrikaner government.[128]

When he read about the Montgomery boycott, Bunting messaged Hugh Brock of *Peace News* about reproducing the comic book for publication in South Africa through Bunting's newspaper, the *New Age*.[129] Bunting wrote on December 6, 1958, "the issue of the Montgomery Bus Boycott is one of great significance to our people and to readers of *New Age*. Only last year 100,000 Africans in the Transvaal walked up to twenty miles a day rather than pay an increase in their bus fare."[130] Bunting was referring to the 1957 Alexandra bus boycott in the Transvaal colony, a protest that illustrates some of the complexities in how South Africans understood the Montgomery boycott in relation to their own struggles.

For decades, Black South Africans in the Transvaal, the Cape, and other colonies had protested the apartheid policies of the Afrikaner government. In the 1940s, these protests coalesced and intensified into a multiracial struggle fueled by labor organizing, the 1946 African mine workers' strike, and the establishments of the Youth League and Women's League in the African National Congress (ANC).[131] In the Transvaal, Black South African women led direct action protests against legislation that required Black people to carry passes with them wherever they traveled, what Gandhi targeted during his organizing on behalf of Indians.[132]

Just as the Montgomery boycott had sprung from years of tireless organizing, the Alexandra boycott was built on decades of struggle. Responding to a bus fare increase, community members formed the Alexandra Peoples' Transport Committee (APTC), with two thousand people voting to boycott the buses "until the old fares were restored."[133] Mary Mkosi participated in the boycott, and she recalled, "we were walking. If you were riding the buses, they were burning the buses! . . . [if the police bothered us,] we took stones and hit them."[134] In the face of state violence, Black South Africans used a bus boycott as one tactic among other forms of resistance, nonviolent and violent. Bunting reflected on the Alexandra boycott by writing, "the people stayed out of the buses for three months until eventually they won a magnificent victory and were able to return to the buses at the old fare."[135] Like in Montgomery, Black South Africans had, through sheer determination, won concessions despite brutal state violence.

Through the FOR comic book, we can more clearly see how Montgomery became a reference point for anti-apartheid activists. The comic book appealed to young Christian missionaries in South Africa, who related to King's Christian upbringing and to his social gospel values. The influence of the social gospel in South Africa has received much less scholarly attention than its influence in the United States South, but from the first decades of the twentieth century Christian missionaries in South Africa reoriented their practices towards reforming society as well as individuals. Richard Elphick argues that many South African missionaries adopted a "Tuskegee" model of the social gospel—borrowed from Booker T. Washington's ideas—which emphasized individual decision-making, reform rather than anti-capitalist revolution, and alliances with "influential and sympathetic Whites."[136] Elphick summarizes the influence of this more conservative brand of the social gospel upon South Africa by writing that, before World War II, "few intellectual developments . . . had greater influence on Black-White relations."[137]

Where Baptist churches were central to how many African Americans learned about the social gospel, in South Africa missionary schools trained generations of political and religious leaders. These schools, which ranged from Dutch Reformed Church (DRC) institutions to non-denominational centers, varied in terms of their political ideology. Some collaborated with the Afrikaner government much more so than others, and DRC theologians contributed to the development of apartheid policies.[138] Other schools from English-speaking missions supported some degree of racial justice by training Black missionaries and ordaining Black clergy.[139] However, by the 1950s and 1960s, almost all missionary schools, regardless of their stance on apartheid, were under attack as the Afrikaner government consolidated power and nationalized the educational system. But by this point, missionary schools in South Africa had already educated generations of Black leaders, including a future president, Nelson Mandela.

While it is unclear how the comic book was distributed throughout South Africa, it is likely that FOR organizers sent it to contacts at missionary schools. In this way, missionary schools linked protest across the Atlantic and assisted the anti-apartheid struggle. The FOR would have had various contacts at Christian schools, and young Black missionaries seem to have been particularly influenced by the comic book. In 1959, the Black youth minister and missionary Jerome Nkosi, who was based in Johannesburg,[140] wrote to the New York branch of FOR, explaining, "I am able to reach scores of our young people with the message of love; and after reading 'Martin Luther King and the Montgomery Story' I feel all the more challenged to do what I can to apply the suggestions outlined in the closing pages to our local situations."[141] Nkosi was inspired by the teachings of nonviolent resistance and by the "method" behind Montgomery. He would have been around the same age as King and probably saw in King's leadership a model for the young students he worked with at his mission. Given that Nkosi was based in the Transvaal, a colony known for its political organizing, it is likely that many students in his congregation participated in the Transvaal boycott and in protests in subsequent years. The comic book, through the FOR's global channels, had directly and indirectly influenced anti-apartheid organizers.

Even as Nkosi read from the comic book, news of Montgomery's influence in South Africa filtered back to organizers in Alabama.

Virginia Durr, the White progressive who supported the boycott's carpools, recalled reading a South African newspaper that referenced King and Parks.[142] One of her contacts in South Africa had likely sent her the article. Through sending and receiving newspaper articles, Durr participated in a transatlantic social network that included Black organizers in Alabama, peace activists in the United Kingdom, and South African correspondents. The Montgomery boycott had, in Durr's view, "spread all over the world."[143]

As ties between Montgomery and South Africa became solidified through the Black press, through letter-writing, and through travel between both places, civil rights leaders in the United States aligned themselves with the growing anti-apartheid movement. During the 1950s, King became one of many prominent African American leaders—including A. Philip Randolph, Bayard Rustin, and Jackie Robinson—to join the anti-apartheid solidarity organization, the American Committee on Africa (ACOA). The ACOA fundraised for South African dissidents and lobbied the United Nations.[144] It also maintained ties with anti-apartheid leaders, including one of Gandhi's children.[145]

Simultaneously, FOR organizers in the United Kingdom communicated with each other about ties between the movement against apartheid and the movement against segregation. A month after Sayre wrote Vera Brittain about the "Christian Gandhi" leading the Montgomery boycott, Brittain responded, writing, "I am much interested in the part which the Fellowship of Reconciliation is playing in the campaign against segregation in the South. We, as you know, have a similar problem in relation to South Africa."[146] Brittain's letter illustrates how news about the Montgomery boycott, and FOR's role in desegregation campaigns, became viewed through the prism of racial justice struggles in other countries. Through its contacts in South Africa and in the United Kingdom, the FOR created networks of solidarity and communication. Struggles in the United States, the United Kingdom, and South Africa became more adjacent and more comparable. Sometimes, the comparisons generated by FOR's comic book highlighted the global nature of the Montgomery struggle, and the global thinking of its organizers. In other respects, FOR's obsession with King flattened the Montgomery boycott, obscuring its most inspirational leaders.

Jo Ann Robinson insisted early on that "the whole world" was watching the boycott, and she was correct.[147] Outside of the South, a world of White FOR activists and Black organizers, of anti-apartheid ministers and pacifists, interpreted the Montgomery boycott. How people learned about the boycott, whether from the comic book or from the Black press, as well as how proximate they were to the struggle, changed how they related to the boycott. As Nkosi's letter indicates, identifying with King's Christianity was particularly important in how the Montgomery boycott became known to anti-apartheid activists. The dissemination of the comic book complicates our understanding of social movements and how they are remembered. Like many struggles, the Montgomery boycott was forged out of local conditions and grassroots organizing. It took on different meanings for organizers around the world, as Paul Stephenson demonstrated in Bristol in 1963.

II

Montgomery and Bristol's Transnational Ties

Contrasted to the mobilization of tens of thousands of Montgomery Blacks, the Bristol boycott transpired without a culture of mass participation. The more behind-the-scenes nature of the Bristol boycott, especially after its first few weeks, nonetheless exemplified the global reach of transnational Black organizing networks. Independent Black and West Indian media outlets, such as Claudia Jones's *West Indian Gazette,* analyzed the Bristol struggle in relation to the racial justice campaigns in the United States South and to the anti-apartheid struggle in South Africa. The Bristol campaign became one chapter in the struggle for freedom from racial oppression, a transnational story in its origins, coverage, and memory.

Long before the bus boycotts in both cities, Montgomery and Bristol were important nodes in transatlantic slavery. By 1860, at least four slave depots operated in Montgomery's city center,[148] and Alabama had become "one of the two largest slave-owning states in America."[149]

Across the Atlantic, the port city of Bristol in southwestern England was also deeply implicated in slavery.[150] Much as Montgomery was never a city with the same size and power as New York,

Bristol was never a metropolitan center like London, Liverpool, or Manchester.

But regionally and nationally, Bristol was an example of how British cities of all sizes depended upon slavery and the slave trade. From the eighteenth through the early nineteenth century, Bristol ships transported more than five hundred thousand slaves from Africa to the Americas to feed the lucrative sugar and palm oil trade.[151] Even through the late eighteenth century, Bristol trailed only London and Liverpool in the number of slave ships that sailed from its ports to Africa.[152] Most of these ships stopped in Jamaica, one of the United Kingdom's most profitable colonies, but other ships sold slaves in the North American colonies, especially South Carolina and Virginia.[153] The M Shed museum in Bristol cites an 1805 slaving voyage of the *Alert* which sold two hundred forty slaves in South Carolina.[154] It is likely that some of these slaves were later moved with their owners' plantations to Alabama or resold to planters there by slave traders.[155] Thus, long before Bristol residents learned about the Montgomery Bus Boycott, the two cities would have been connected through the brutal linkages of transatlantic slavery.

Montgomery and Bristol were cities with very different histories of race, racism, and migration. By 1955, African Americans made up some 40 percent of Montgomery population.[156] Many were descendants of slaves and sharecroppers. In Bristol, by contrast, in 1963 Afro-Caribbeans were some 7,000 people in a city of 350,000, just 2 percent of the total population.[157] Many Afro-Caribbeans, who referred to themselves as West Indians, were also descendants of slaves, but, unlike African Americans in Montgomery, most had only lived in Bristol for a short time.

Other migrants from South Asia and Africa had also made Bristol their home. Since at least the seventeenth century, South

Asians had stayed in Bristol during tours of the United Kingdom. By the early twentieth century, the "largest foreign student body at British universities were Indian students."[158] In 1930, Bristol University had twenty-eight Indian students. Indian and South Asian migrants continued to arrive in Bristol through the 1963 boycott, becoming prominent doctors, politicians, and activists in the city. Pakistani migrants who arrived in the United Kingdom as seamen during World War II were stationed in port cities throughout the country, including in Bristol. According to the BBC, the 1963 protest coincided with a peak of Pakistani migration to the United Kingdom.[159]

While less present in the Bristol archives, Black African migrants also formed small communities. The long history of African communities in Britain has been documented by scholars such as Peter Aspinall and Martha Chinouya. After fighting in both World War I and World War II, some Black Africans stayed in the United Kingdom. Aspinall and Chinouya explain that "colonies of seamen" developed in Britain's seaport towns such as Cardiff and Liverpool.[160] As a major port city, Bristol likely also became a home for Black African seamen and their families in the post-World War II era. The presence of South Asian, Black African, and West Indian migrants to Bristol during the postwar period complicates a Black-White racial binary and illustrates the larger significance behind the city's treatment of its non-White residents.

The Bristol boycott unfolded in a city that was home to people with various racial and ethnic backgrounds. Correspondingly, migrants were accorded different political rights and enjoyed various levels of racial privilege depending on many factors, including the color of their skin, their birthplace within the British Empire and its colonies, their class, and their level of education. The particular ways in which West Indians faced racial discrimination in Bristol, treatment that paralleled or diverged from the discrimination experienced by South Asians and Black Africans, must be further explored.

Ken Pryce's *Endless Pressure* is a helpful starting point for learning about Bristol's West Indian community.[161] While small, the West Indian population in Bristol was growing quickly in the early 1950s, due in part to divergent migration policy in the United States compared with the United Kingdom. In 1948, the British government passed its Nationality Act, which allowed individuals in Commonwealth countries to migrate to the United Kingdom and become citizens. Meanwhile, the United States government imposed the restrictive McCarran-Walter Act of 1952, which arose during a period of McCarthyism and reintroduced a "national origins" quota system for immigrants.[162] Paul Stephenson would later identify the Act, along with widespread unemployment, as one of the key causes of migration from the Caribbean to the United Kingdom.[163] Taking advantage of this opening, the June 1948 journey of the SS *Empire Windrush* from Jamaica to the United Kingdom, with around five hundred West Indians, marked a period of "mass migration to the 'mother country.'"[164]

Some migrants were received more favorably than others by White Britons. Stephenson noted that "in 1954 the Government appointed five internal investigation studies into commonwealth migration but none into Irish or Italian immigration,"[165] despite Irish and Italian immigration dwarfing that from the West Indies, South Asia, and other parts of the Commonwealth. Given the long history of British subjugation of Irish people, the fact that migration from Ireland did not cause as much consternation as that from the Caribbean illustrates how Britons in the post-World War II era increasingly defined the favorability of migrants depending on the color of their skin.

Racism and xenophobia in British politics implicated Labour as well as Conservative politicians and leaders. In 1948, Labour MPs warned Prime Minister Clement Attlee that "an influx of colored people domiciled here is likely to impair the harmony, strength and cohesion of our public and social life and to cause discord and unhappiness."[166] In hindsight, the 1948 Nationality Act marked not a new era of tolerance towards non-White migrants from the Commonwealth but instead a period when white supremacy became mobilized politically. White politicians were concerned that migration by people of color from Britain's former colonies would erode the Whiteness of the United Kingdom as a whole.

WEST INDIAN CIVIC LIFE IN BRISTOL

In the post-World War II era, fear of non-White migrants manifested itself in countless color bars and restrictions on employment and housing across the United Kingdom. Roy Hackett migrated to the United Kingdom from Jamaica in 1952 and arrived in Bristol in 1957.[167] He recalled that "it was terrible for Black people in Bristol in the '50s. We were treated like second-class citizens."[168]

In response to increased West Indian migration, Bristol's industries and unions closed ranks, limiting job opportunities for people of color. The Transport and General Workers' Union (TGWU)—a trade union made up of all transportation workers in the city, with members from the docks, buses, and railways—feared competition for jobs. Bristol's color bar began in 1955 after a TGWU vote allowed West Indians in the maintenance shop but not in public-facing roles as drivers or conductors.[169] The vote paralleled union policies in other parts of the country. In some cases, transportation unions and bus companies implemented "quotas of immigrant workers."[170] While nationally the TGWU maintained a policy against racial discrimination, in practice, and at the regional level, a system of de facto racial segregation developed.[171]

Bristol also maintained openly racist housing policies that forced West Indians to live in a small sector of the city, the St. Paul's neighborhood. As one measure of racism in Bristol society, a 1963 survey found that just 3 percent of landladies would "consent even to consider a colored student as a possible lodger."[172] A 1965 study by the sociologist Anthony Richmond found that 60 percent of individuals agreed or strongly agreed with the statement, "colored immigrants have made the housing shortage in Bristol much worse."[173] These findings suggest how housing and employment became the principal ways in which racism and xenophobia manifested themselves in Bristol.

In response to overt and covert hostility, West Indians began organizing on behalf of their communities. Founded in the early 1950s, the West Indian Association (WIA) served as a hub for those seeking job advancement and educational opportunities. A 1963 newsletter described the Association as "gradualist,"[174] perhaps analogous to the National Urban League in the United States, which generally avoided direct action protests. Roy Hackett, along with several West Indians, including Owen Henry, Audley Evans, and Prince Brown, responded to the need for a more militant organization by forming the West Indian Development Council (WIDC).[175]

Due in part to gendered migratory patterns to the United Kingdom, but also due to men being privileged by historical archives, West Indian women have not appeared in most sources on the 1963 boycott. As Nancy Foner and others have pointed out, during the 1950s and 1960s most West Indian migrants to the United Kingdom were men.[176] About 70 percent of migrants to the United Kingdom 1952–1954 were men, and around 60 percent in 1960. Foner explains that "in most cases, there was simply not enough money for the whole family to emigrate to Britain together, and men, as the main expected family providers, probably received preference in raising the rather considerable funds to pay for the passage."[177] Ceri Peach, who Foner cites, has come to similar conclusions.[178] The WIDC was led by men, but it certainly was also composed of West Indian women who worked without media attention like Jo Ann Robinson and Rosa Parks in Montgomery.

Paul Stephenson, who would become the focus of media interest, joined the WIDC as one of its first members. He arrived in Bristol just a year before the boycott but quickly became a well-known public figure. A 1962 article described Stephenson as a "full-time youth leader," but misidentified him as "a West Indian."[179] He had been born in Britain and raised in an almost exclusively White community in Essex, northeast of London. His father was West African, and his mother was White and had been born in the United Kingdom.[180] After serving in the Royal Air Force (RAF) in Germany, Stephenson studied in a "community work course" at West Hill College in Birmingham, moving into a life of organizing and social work.[181] Similar to Rosa Parks's work in the U.S. NAACP, Stephenson became a youth organizer,[182] and he taught at a secondary school in Bristol's St. Paul's neighborhood where he spoke with students and their parents.[183] It was here he would have interacted with young West Indian immigrants.

Reporting on Struggles for Freedom in the UK and the USA

Stephenson joined the WIDC at a time when struggles for freedom were being compared and connected across the Atlantic. Claudia Jones, a Trinidadian woman who migrated to Britain in 1955, increasingly publicized the connections between the civil rights movement in the United States and movements for racial justice in the United Kingdom. In Jones's *West Indian Gazette,* articles from the Jamaican daily *The Gleaner* were reprinted alongside stories from African American newspapers.[184]

Due in part to this coverage, Martin Luther King Jr. became a widely known Black leader across the Atlantic. A series of articles in the *Gazette* described King's 1961 visit to the United Kingdom, noting that "no recent visit has so stirred the conscience of Britain as that of Dr. Martin Luther King, thirty-two-year-old pastor of Atlanta, Georgia, of Montgomery Bus Boycott and 'Freedom Riders' fame."[185] While misidentifying King as a Freedom Rider, the reporting came at a crucial political moment in Britain. The 1962 Commonwealth Immigration Act restricted migration to the United Kingdom by people of color, forcing prospective migrants to apply for work vouchers.[186] The *Daily Gleaner* and the *Gazette* quickly saw through the Act for what it was: a color bar on migration.[187]

While Black Britons saw clear differences between Jim Crow legislation in the United States South and de facto segregation in the United Kingdom, in the realm of immigration policy, it was more obvious how racial discrimination was taking root in society and government. Reporting on the U.S. civil rights movement by outlets such as the *Gazette* was a warning to Black Britons of the need for forward-thinking organizing on behalf of immigrant and West Indian communities.

Such reporting has been described by the historian Nick Juravich as an example of how British organizers "transplanted tactics" from the United States to Britain. Juravich notes that "tactics, rhetoric, and strategy that were considered quintessentially 'American' with respect to civil rights protest were reproduced in Britain."[188] Connections between the two countries were widespread, epitomized by military alliances during World War II that saw many African American soldiers stationed in the United Kingdom.

Claudia Jones, second from left under banner, leads an anti-racist march in Notting Hill, London, in the 1960s. (Courtesy West Indian Gazette)

These links ran so deep that later in the 1960s, the sit-in movement, ignited by African American students in Greensboro, North Carolina, and popularized by the Student Nonviolent Coordinating Committee (SNCC), turned into "drink-ins." Black Britons protested racial discrimination in pubs by sitting at bars and refusing to leave unless they were served a drink. In 1965, Paul Stephenson exposed a color bar at the Bay House pub in Bristol by adopting this strategy. Arrested for his "drink-in," Stephenson won widespread media coverage for the action and, eventually, a successful legal challenge against the pub.[189]

The explosion of interest in racial justice movements was not only a case of Black Britons looking towards the United States for inspiration. Kennetta Hammond Perry and Marc Matera have written about the emergence of London as a space for transnational Black organizing. During the interwar period, Afro-Caribbeans and African Americans, including Eslanda Goode Robeson, Amy Ashwood Garvey, George Padmore, and CLR James, generated political spaces in London that afforded Black people respite and community.[190] Some of these same networks facilitated renewed communication between the United States and Britain during the postwar era.

In 1963, the U.S. civil rights movement became an even more common topic of debate in independent and mainstream media in the United Kingdom. Even conservative publications, such as the *Daily Mail,* maintained a consensus support for King as an "integration leader."[191] In June, the *Gazette* published front-page articles on the struggle for freedom in Birmingham, Alabama, writing that "West Indians, Africans, Asians and other democratic forces who abhor color bar as inimical to democracy can show their solidarity with the Negro people by sending a message of support to them."[192] The color bar became one of the primary ways in which British newspapers related to the struggles in the United States South. While the kind of color bar was different in Alabama as compared to Bristol, one de jure, the other de facto, British and American activists saw color bars in both locations as examples of the transnational nature of white supremacy.

Stephenson understood that one way in which he could build support and sympathy for the struggle in Bristol was to connect the boycott to the United States civil rights movement. By making such a comparison present in the minds of British people, he could create a moral quandary. If Britons believed that their country was more democratic along racial issues than the United States, then the Bristol boycott represented a grave threat to this halcyon vision.

He was also raising the specter of the United Kingdom's complicity with slavery. The protest called into question a myth of moral superiority that some Britons had maintained concerning their country's ties to slavery. Since most slaves in the British Empire had labored on plantations in the West Indies and in locations away from the "homeland," British people could in some ways ignore and de-emphasize the centrality of slavery to the British political economy. Many planters who owned massive plantations in Jamaica and other Caribbean islands governed their estates from afar so they could deny personal responsibility even as they profited from slave labor and financed transatlantic slavery.

The increasingly visible reality of West Indians migrating to Bristol and to other cities—many descendants of former slaves—meant that some British people might have to reckon with their country's history of slavery and colonialism. West Indian migration forced some awareness on the part of White Britons about legacies of racial oppression. Meanwhile, West Indian migrants sought a better life in the United Kingdom precisely because slavery had under-developed the Caribbean and contributed towards its economic and political precariousness, a realization that Stephenson likely understood would generate sympathy for the West Indians participating in the Bristol boycott.

LEARNING ABOUT MONTGOMERY

Stephenson did not visit Alabama until 1964. Claire Mansour argues that Stephenson was a "relational tie bridging the gap between the two movements," but she does not explore where he first learned about the Montgomery movement.[193] Possibly, Stephenson read Alistair Cooke's 1956 articles in the *Manchester Guardian,* but it is as likely that he read the *Gazette.* In any case, at some point during the late 1950s, Stephenson became captivated by the leadership of King and the courageous action of Parks.

In a filmed 2009 interview, Stephenson explained, "I wanted to know how best I could bring this dramatically before the public, in a way that would capture the imagination of not only the Black community but far wider."[194] He recalled, "the idea came to me . . . a boycott. Luther King had boycotted buses in Alabama over Black people being forced to stay in the back of the buses. So I thought we would do the same tactic, this time over employment."[195] It would be a mistake to suggest that Stephenson was the only leader of the Bristol bus boycott. While many have focused on his leadership, this is partly due to limited source material. There have been no book-length studies of the Bristol boycott, and most have relied heavily on a single source: Madge Dresser's 1986 *Black and White on the Buses.* Dresser's detailed account surveys the day-to-day activities of the Bristol boycott, focusing on Stephenson and several other leaders. While there are numerous articles from regional and national press on the boycott, these articles represent mostly how White British men interpreted the boycott.

Whereas the Montgomery boycott was predicated on the mass participation of Black citizens, and organized through a culture of mass meetings, the Bristol boycott proceeded along different lines of attack. With a much smaller West Indian population in Bristol, boycott organizers knew they could not rely on public demonstrations to pressure legislators. Instead, organizers appealed to White leaders within and outside of the city for their support. In both boycotts, though, there was a precipitating event that mobilized support for the boycott and focused attention on racial injustices. The case of Rosa Parks is well-known, but the case of Guy Bailey in Bristol is much less so.

A Test Case: Guy Bailey

Migrating from Jamaica to Bristol in 1961, Bailey was just nineteen years old in 1963. Stephenson taught Bailey in a night class in Bristol, and he realized that his student would make an ideal test case for the color bar.[196] Bailey was a "Boy's Brigade Officer," a member of the local cricket club, a warehouse worker, and a part-time student.[197] His work ethic and the status afforded him as a member of various local institutions ensured that he would be viewed as more respectable to White people and West Indians in Bristol.

Stephenson called the Bristol Omnibus Company asking about a job vacancy for a bus driver and setting up an interview for Bailey. The bus company confirmed to Stephenson that there were vacancies, but, once it found out that Bailey was West Indian, canceled the interview.[198] Stephenson then spoke with the bus company's general manager, Ian Patey, who told him that the company did ban "colored labor."[199] In response to Patey's defense of the color bar, the WIDC mobilized support for a boycott by holding a press conference where Stephenson called for a boycott of the buses until the color bar in employment was overturned.[200]

Owen Henry, a member of the WIDC, recalled the significance of the press conference. He explained that afterwards the WIDC invited press to take photos of him standing at the back of a Bristol bus. The visual symbolism worked in various ways. In Bristol, the back of the bus was where bus conductors stood.[201]

By standing in the back of the bus, Henry created a "rival geography," signaling to onlookers that West Indians deserved the visibility and freedom that employment on the buses could bring. The term rival geographies, coined by Edward Said and defined by the historian Stephanie Camp as "alternative ways of knowing and using plantation and Southern space that conflicted with planters' ideals and demands," also applies to this context.[202] Plantations in the U.S. South attempted to create rigid forms of spatial control, limiting where slaves could move and travel. Plantations were spaces policed by White overseers. Metaphorically speaking, Bristol's buses represented a similar kind of spatial control in the city's racial imaginary. The buses were patrolled by White conductors and drivers, and, in this imaginary, they were populated only by White passengers. Of course, in practice, West Indian, South Asian, and other people of color also rode Bristol buses, and their increasingly common presence on public transit destabilized this imaginary. When Bristol newspapers snapped photos of Henry in the bus, they published a new, rival geography and a new future for the city.

The press conference won increased coverage. Over the next four months, local, regional, and national newspapers including the *Western Daily Press,* the *Bristol Evening Post,* and the *Guardian* closely monitored the bus company and the boycott. The *Evening Post* led coverage by publishing editorials critical of the bus company and of the TGWU. An anonymous editorial from April 30, 1963, argued that Bristol would receive "adverse publicity" from the color bar. The editorial cited that "Mr. Ian Patey, the company's general manager, claimed today that a mixed labor force would worsen labor supply because of the prejudice among White people." It added, "but what of the bus crews whose prejudice virtually dictates company policy? What are trade union leaders doing to get the race virus out of the systems of their rank and file?"[203]

One of Patey's chief defenses of the color bar was that the TGWU had forced bus company management to enact it. The TGWU was irate upon hearing about the editorial, and it claimed that the color bar had been established by management. The truth was that both bus management and the rank and file enacted and maintained the color bar. In 1955, the color bar had been established by the

TGWU, and Dresser argues that the union "did not seem to treat the existence of racial discrimination as a matter of urgency."[204] By not resisting the color bar, the union ensured its survival. At the same time, bus management actively perpetuated the bar through its discriminatory hiring practices and its decision to only hire White bus conductors and drivers.

A Boycott Without Boycotters?

While many West Indians supported the aims of the boycott, most continued to ride Bristol buses to work and to travel around the city. An April 30, 1963, article quoted a boycott leader reporting 100 percent support "from the city's seven thousand West Indians."[205] This was probably a significant exaggeration. Other sources suggest that only a small minority of West Indians boycotted the buses. In June, the IRR reported that "some forty of the city's estimated seven thousand West Indians turned out in answer to Mr. Stephenson's call to picket a Bristol church but the bus boycott was reported to be negligible."[206]

Partly, the paltry turnout for the boycott reflected the conservative role of churches in Bristol. In contrast to Black Baptist churches in Montgomery, the Bristol Council of Churches accused a "small group of West Indians professing to be representative" of creating "what may prove to be an extended racial conflict."[207] Church leaders distanced themselves from a protest that they felt aggravated rather than uncovered racism and discrimination against West Indians. It is unclear whether other religious groups in Bristol—Muslim West Indians or people with indigenous Caribbean faiths—aligned themselves with the protest, but Christian leaders generally opposed the movement.

At least in the initial weeks of the boycott, direct action protests initiated by Stephenson, Hackett, and others suggest that community members were fairly supportive of the aims of the boycott, with some putting their jobs and bodies on the line. Roy Hackett recalls blockading the Bristol bus station, and at least one mass march both paralleled the direct action tactics of the U.S. civil rights movement and suggested cross-racial solidarity between West Indians and White university students in Bristol.[208] On May 1, a group of around one hundred mostly White Bristol students marched from the University of Bristol to the bus station and local headquarters of the TGWU, passing through the city center.[209] The students carried banners reading "Shame On Our Bus Company" and "Boycott Bristol Buses." As they marched through downtown Bristol, bus crews heckled them, but the marchers reached the bus station, where they delivered a "protest letter" to Ron Nethercott, the regional secretary of the TGWU.[210]

Paul Stephenson then addressed the marchers, explaining that "people are now saying that this is worse in Bristol than it is in the Deep South of America."[211] Clearly, for Stephenson, the "Deep South" was a warning to White people and West Indians: end the color bar, or else see Bristol descend into the social upheaval of Birmingham, Alabama.

From their position within the Black Atlantic, West Indian newspapers reported on developments in Bristol, ensuring that the boycott reached a far greater audience than Stephenson may have imagined. In Jamaica, the newly independent country that sent many migrants to Bristol, local newspapers reported on the movement, led by the century-old *Daily Gleaner*. At some point during the spring of 1963, Margaret Batt read about the Bristol boycott in a Jamaican newspaper. She had lived in Bristol and then moved to Jamaica, and she wrote to the *Bristol Evening Post,* "'Is our criticism of South Africa's policy, in these circumstances, not merely a case of 'the kettle calling the pan sooty'? I appeal to fellow Bristolians to join the West Indians in their boycott of the buses."[212]

Negotiating a Settlement

One of the main differences between the Montgomery and Bristol boycotts was in how negotiations proceeded. In Montgomery, the Black lawyer Fred D. Gray—just twenty-five years old during the boycott—led legal representation on behalf of King and the MIA. Throughout the boycott, he defended Rosa Parks, Claudette Colvin, and many others from baseless charges, mass indictments, and the threat of long jail sentences. When these tactics of suppression failed, it was thanks in part to Gray's steadfast legal work. Gray also filed the petition that challenged state laws mandating segregation on Alabama buses, the *Browder v. Gayle* civil litigation that eventually made its way to the U.S. Supreme Court.[213]

Gray's significant role in the successful outcome of the boycott, which he detailed in his memoir *Bus Ride to Justice,* played out in courtrooms and attorney's offices—spaces in Alabama and in many other parts of the country that had been constructed and maintained to preserve and protect white supremacy. Going back to the Black Codes following the Civil War, when free Black people were prevented from fully participating in social and political democracy in the South, the Alabama legal system and its many courthouses were spaces that protected civil rights for White people, and particularly White men, but systematically erased civil rights for others. Historically, from Reconstruction through the post-World War II era, these were institutions where racial segregation had been upheld and entrenched. It was quite telling that four months into the boycott the Alabama legislature convened in Montgomery over the "race issue," and introduced new pro-segregation bills.[214] White legislators, shocked by the persistence of the boycott, responded by attempting to further restrict Black political expression and freedom.

By entering and disrupting the legal system in Alabama, Gray challenged the edifice of white supremacy. The legal system in Montgomery responded with delay and diversion, with counter lawsuits and mass arrests, but, eventually, the persistence of the boycott and its legal challenge succeeded. In November 1956, the United States Supreme Court affirmed the boycott, effectively ending segregation on Montgomery buses as soon as the mailed order reached city officials the next month.[215]

As legal cases worked from the state to the federal level, Black people stayed off the buses for 382 straight days. In Bristol, by contrast, there is little evidence that the boycott continued as negotiations proceeded. As there was no British state or local law protecting racial segregation, just the proclivities and power of the Bristol bus company, negotiations proceeded without the involvement of British courts and without formal legal representation.

However, in the months after British media focused on the U.S. civil rights movement, Bristol also became a topic of national news and interest. During the summer of 1963, comment on the Bristol boycott came from politicians led by Sir Learie Constantine. He was a well-known ex-cricket player who became the Caribbean High Commissioner for Trinidad and Tobago, akin to an ambassador in the context of United States diplomacy.[216] Somewhat fortuitously, Constantine visited Bristol for a cricket match on May 4, 1963, and, upon learning about the boycott, he wrote to the Bristol Omnibus Company (BOC) about refusing to hire Black workers.[217] An influential national politician, he realized that Patey and the BOC would not reconsider their position, so he focused on the Transport Holding Company (THC) in London. Created by the Transport Act of 1962, the government-owned THC regulated railways and bus companies across the country, giving it great control over Bristol bus management.[218]

Through Constantine's communications, the THC began pressuring Patey into negotiations, while other politicians also supported the boycott. Anthony Wedgwood Benn, a former MP for Bristol South-East, "cabled a message of support" to Stephenson and wrote "several articles condemning the color bar." In London, the Labour leader Harold Wilson, prime minister in 1964, pointed out the hypocrisy of criticizing "racial intolerance in South Africa and not in Bristol."[219] Together, local and national leaders helped draw attention to the situation in Bristol, but some West Indians resented what they felt were unfair attacks.

Bill Smith, chair of the Bristol WIA, issued a joint statement with TGWU's regional secretary Ron Nethercott in which they suggested Stephenson and the boycott had inflamed racial tensions. The statement called for negotiations "without heat or emotion," bemoaning attacks on the bus company.[220] They drew on a particular form of respectability politics.[221] Smith felt that the boycott had destroyed more gradualist efforts on the part of the TGWU to negotiate with management to allow Black bus drivers. He said that "negotiations got colored men into the garages and would have got them onto the buses."[222] Whether these negotiations were happening, and how quickly they were moving, is hard to tell.

In her dissertation, Rosie Wild, a historian of British Black Power, concludes that "because there had been so little grassroots support for the boycott the local Black communities were neither more politicized nor united as a result of the campaign." Wild adds that "given the limited impact of the boycott and slow pace of progress after the color bar's end, it is possible that the WIA's gradualist approach may have achieved the same results, as it angrily claimed."[223] Yet the gradualist approach offered by Smith could well have dragged on for years, at a time when West Indians badly needed jobs and housing.

Through Stephenson and Constantine's action, the THC quickly sided against the color bar. On May 7, Philip Warter, chair of the THC, announced that in the future "there will be no color bar on Bristol buses at all . . . It just could not be tolerated."[224] Of course, the color bar had been tolerated for eight years, but Warter's declaration forced Patey to open negotiations with the TGWU, a decision that otherwise may have taken many more years. Wild concludes that "it was, therefore, at the level of national politics and international diplomatic relations, as well as local and national news coverage, that the campaign to revoke the color bar was won."[225]

Considering the role of Constantine, along with national leaders in Britain, it is clear that Stephenson's main victory during the boycott was not so much mobilizing local support, but instead generating international attention through leveraging government contacts. In this way, Stephenson accomplished what King understood so intimately: media coverage could highlight racial injustice and increase political influence and impact. As Stephenson remembered in 2009, Bristol "became international. This was April 1963. Jamaica, Trinidad had just become independent countries. So their high commissions wanted to become involved, to say that we've got to look after our nationals."[226] Diplomatic and national pressure on Bristol forced the bus company to the negotiating table, more so than any one march or blockade.

DREAMING OF RESOLUTIONS

Fittingly, negotiations between the bus company and the TGWU concluded on August 28, 1963. The day of the historic March on Washington, as King delivered his iconic "I Have a Dream" speech, the color bar ended with a short statement of resolution.

Following "months of secret negotiations between the two sides,"[227] the agreement between the Bristol Omnibus Company and the TGWU called for the "employment of suitable colored workers," and Patey added that "this means full integration without regard to race, color, or creed."[228] The agreement had been endorsed by five hundred members of the TGWU.

In response, Stephenson wrote an op-ed thanking "the many hundreds of people" who supported the "struggle against color discrimination."[229] The first person of color to become a bus conductor in Bristol was, in fact, not West Indian. In mid-September, Raghbir Singh, an Indian-born Sikh man who had lived in Bristol since 1959, became a bus conductor as a test that the color bar was no longer in place.[230] Giving up his higher-paying job as an engineer fitter, Singh said he "applied for the job to see if the bus company kept to its word," thus expressing solidarity with West Indians.[231] The hiring of Singh suggested how the Bristol movement benefited not just West Indians but people of color from various ethnic backgrounds. Shortly after Singh was hired, two Jamaican and two Pakistani men became conductors.[232] The Bristol boycott generated new forms of cross-racial solidarity, a sign the protest was more effective in politicizing and uniting local communities than is sometimes imagined.

The Bristol boycott symbolizes one afterlife of the Montgomery movement. Although the political situation facing West Indians in Bristol was quite different than the racial segregation that African Americans contested in Montgomery, Stephenson nonetheless understood how America's racial politics could stand as a warning to White and West Indian Britons. By invoking the racism of Alabama, and by also recalling the inspiration of Rosa Parks and Martin Luther King Jr., Stephenson's leadership of the Bristol protest connected two bus protests across the Atlantic. At a fundamental level, Stephenson expressed solidarity with African Americans, a kind of solidarity that highlighted the ties between people on opposite coasts of the Black Atlantic.

If the end of the color bar on Bristol buses represented an important short-term victory, then it is much harder to assess how this struggle influenced racial politics in Britain as a whole. The 1965 and 1968 Race Relations Acts prohibited racial discrimination in public places and in accommodation, with the 1968 act banning employment discrimination. Madge Dresser explains that one might conclude that the Bristol campaign "helped to raise the consciousness of Parliament . . . to take a stand against racial discrimination. But if we do, we should also keep in mind that the Race Relations Acts have been seen by some commentators as merely a sop to make immigration restrictions more palatable."[233] In 1968, Parliament passed the Commonwealth Immigrants Act, restricting the rights of Commonwealth citizens attempting to migrate to the United Kingdom. The Act targeted British nationals in Africa, particularly in Kenya, who were arriving in the United Kingdom in increasing numbers.[234] Even as the UK banned racial discrimination domestically, its immigration legislation suggested that the battle for racial justice remained ongoing.

Conclusions

In 1964, a year after the Bristol boycott ended, Paul Stephenson sojourned across the Atlantic, invited by the NAACP on a lecture tour to New York, Philadelphia, Baltimore, Washington, D.C., and, finally, Alabama.[235] During his six-week trip, he spoke about his involvement in the Bristol boycott and about racial politics in Britain. In Montgomery, he may have stayed with Virginia and Clifford Durr, the well-known White progressives who supported the boycott and who hosted many Britons on their trips to the region.[236]

Jo Ann Robinson had already left Montgomery. In 1960, Alabama State College (ASC) students had staged sit-ins at Montgomery restaurants and lunch counters as part of a national wave of student protests against racial segregation. Alabama Governor John Patterson responded by ordering the expulsion of the students and the firing of at least a dozen faculty who supported the protests, including Robinson, Mary Fair Burks, and Lawrence Reddick.[237] Robinson moved to Grambling College in Louisiana and a year later to Los Angeles, California, where she published a memoir and taught until retirement. She passed away in 1992.[238]

Rosa Parks also left Montgomery shortly after the boycott concluded. In 1957, after facing racist attacks and intimidation, she moved to Detroit in search of stable employment. Although the MIA declared August 5, 1957, as "Rosa Parks Day" and held a celebration before her departure, Montgomery organizers had failed to secure a paid position for Parks within the SCLC or in another organization. She and her husband moved to Virginia, where she worked at Hampton Institute, before relocating to Detroit. In 1965, she campaigned for John Conyers in his successful bid for the U.S. House, after which she worked in his office until her retirement in 1988. She died in 2005.[239]

After his travels through the South in 1964, Stephenson visited Jamaica before returning to the United Kingdom.[240] For the rest of his adult life, he continued to organize in community groups, eventually helping form the Bristol Black Archives Partnership in 2009 to preserve Bristol's Black history.[241] The same year, he was awarded the Order of the British Empire. Stephenson's involvement in Community Relations Councils, a state-run system, signified one approach to organizing, but radical Black leaders avoided partnering with the British government. Similar to splits in the United States, such as when the Black Panther Party emerged from SNCC, fissures in struggles for racial justice developed as the United Kingdom became a hub for global Black Power.[242]

The connections and disconnections between civil rights struggles in the United States and in the United Kingdom, as well as ties between these movements and the anti-apartheid struggle, suggest a complex web of social movements. Future scholarship must contend not only with the development of global Black Power, which has become an exciting area of research, but also with transnational ties during the freedom struggles of the 1950s and 1960s. As Nick Juravich notes, "the history of Black Power in Britain . . . has been far more extensively researched and reported than the earlier period of civil rights protest."[243] There remain opportunities for scholarship joining the post-war period with late-1960s Black Power. Through ideological exchange, as well as mass migration, African Americans and Black Britons shared tactics and generated new alliances, changes chronicled by intrepid Black editors and writers.

More recently, the toppling of Confederate memorials in the United States has inspired parallel efforts in the United Kingdom to take down statues of slave traders. In 2020, activists in Bristol toppled the statue of Edward Colston near the city's harbor, and some have called for a statue of Stephenson to fill its place.[244] Across the Atlantic, expressions of solidarity in the fight against white supremacy continue to inspire new protests and new leaders.

There remain opportunities for smaller memorials, such as the plaque below in the Bristol bus station, to link protest across the Atlantic. When struggles for freedom are connected transnationally, instead of siloed in a national or state framework, the radical imaginations of activists can be understood and appreciated. The bus station plaque is titled, "The Bristol Bus Boycott 1963." But to account for global connections it could be titled "The Bristol Bus Boycott 1963, in Solidarity with Montgomery." Of course, symbolic gestures of solidarity are never sufficient in movements for justice and freedom, and social movements must continue to create concrete alliances.

The Montgomery Bus Boycott can be understood as a local and a global struggle. Montgomery organizers recognized that their boycott was occurring during a period of anticolonialism around the world, and that their freedom was linked to that of others. In this way, the story of the Montgomery movement confirms histories of global anti-imperial solidarities. The Montgomery boycott offers evidence that, on the level of grassroots politics as well as on the level of Bandung diplomacy, African American organizers related their struggles to anticolonialism. The boycott underscores the importance of scholarship that highlights everyday expressions of anticolonial solidarities, not just transcendent moments of collaboration such as Bandung.

Through a commitment to nonviolence, Montgomery organizers connected the tactics of their movement to the independence struggle in India and to anti-apartheid movements in South Africa. The impact and influence of Gandhian nonviolence in Montgomery was highlighted by the venerable pacifist organization, the Fellowship of Reconciliation. FOR advisors made the unexpected decision to publish what became an internationally distributed comic book, a guidebook on nonviolence that took on a life of its own. In the years following the conclusion of the Montgomery boycott, the movement gained a mythical status through this comic book, as readers in the United Kingdom and in South Africa learned about the young Gandhian prophet, Martin Luther King Jr. The FOR comic book centered King as the protagonist of the boycott, obscuring the key leadership of Black women but highlighting the Gandhi-King connection. King's upbringing in the Baptist church appealed to the religious convictions of Christian South Africans, especially young missionaries. More recently, the comic book was translated into Arabic and Farsi, and organizers carried it at protests during the Arab Spring, a sign of its enduring influence.[245]

The FOR comic book illustrates how media, art, and literature can publicize and sometimes distort social movements. Despite its historical erasures, the comic book exposed more people to King's life and to the story of the boycott. The transnational Black press also reported on the Montgomery struggle to readers in the West Indies and in the United Kingdom. Through her articles, Claudia Jones viewed the Bristol and Montgomery movements as struggles challenging white supremacy in both countries, connections that

*Memorial in today's Bristol bus station to the Boycott of 1963.
On the left of the plaque, there are images of protestors walking
through the center of the city carrying signs. On the far right is a
depiction of Raghbir Singh, the Sikh man who became the first
person of color hired as a bus conductor after the end of the color
bar. (Plaque created by Mike Baker. Photo by Cole Manley.)*

Paul Stephenson intuited as well. Stephenson was inspired by what
he learned about the Montgomery movement, and he used the
boycott as an important reference point in the struggle for justice
in Bristol.

In the ways in which it was imagined, the Montgomery movement grew to mean many different things to many different people.
Through solidarity, organizers in Bristol and in South Africa could
apply the lessons of Montgomery to their own political environ-
ments. The symbols of Montgomery were varied. Some organizers

like Stephenson embraced the person in the back of the bus. Others were inspired by the ethic of love, or by the Christian upbringing of King. But through these symbols, the Montgomery boycott played out in people's imaginations in faraway places. The stories and legends of the boycott—its mythology—amplified its global impact and its relevance to social movements elsewhere.[246]

Bibliography

Primary Sources

Archival Materials

ADAH. Alabama Department of Archives and History. Montgomery, Alabama.

    Inez Baskin papers.

    James Elisha Folsom papers, 1938–1981.

    Juliette Hampton Morgan papers.

    Lila Bess Olin Morgan family papers.

    Lyon Addition to Durr papers.

    Virginia Foster Durr papers.

ASU. Alabama State University. Levi Watkins Learning Center Archives and Special Collections. Montgomery, Alabama.

    Montgomery Bus Boycott Newspaper Clippings Collection, 1955–1956.

    Montgomery Improvement Association collection.

ARC. Amistad Research Center. Tulane University. New Orleans, Louisiana.

    Preston and Bonita Valien Papers, 1932–1996.

BA. Bristol Archives. Bristol, England.

    Paul Stephenson Collection.

Lurel Roy Hackett Collection.

Bristol Omnibus Company Collection.

Hansard. "Transport Holding Company Bill." Accessed 31 March 2020, https://hansard.parliament.uk/commons/1968–01-16/debates/eb0a4b40-d737-432d-b8b5-8c472e16f863/TransportHoldingCompanyBill.

Institute of Race Relations. London, United Kingdom. Accessed 12 September 2019. http://www.irr.org.uk/resources/bhc/.

The Institute of Race Relations Newsletter, 1960–1965.

The West Indian Gazette, 1959–1965.

"West Indian Gazette and Afro-Asian-Caribbean News | Institute of Race Relations."

King, Martin Luther, Clayborne Carson, Ralph E. Luker, Peter Holloran, and Penny A. Russell. The Papers of Martin Luther King, Jr., Volume IV: Symbol of the Movement, January 1957–December 1958. University of California Press, 1992.

MLKI. The Martin Luther King, Jr. Research and Education Institute. Stanford University, CA.

"An Autobiography of Religious Development." The Martin Luther King, Jr., Research and Education Institute. https://kinginstitute.stanford.edu/king-papers/documents/autobiography-religious-development.

Jo Ann Robinson. https://kinginstitute.stanford.edu/encyclopedia/robinson-jo-ann-gibson

Parks, Rosa. https://kinginstitute.stanford.edu/encyclopedia/parks-rosa.

"King's World House," February 20, 2019, https://kinginstitute.stanford.edu/liberation-curriculum/lesson-plans/activities/kings-world-house.

Schomburg Center for Research in Black Culture, The New York Public Library.

George R. Metcalf papers.

SCPC. Swarthmore College Peace Collection. Swarthmore, Pennsylvania.

Fellowship of Reconciliation Records.

John Nevin Sayre Papers.

Online Newspapers and Periodicals

"Archives | Afro." Accessed 2 November 2019. https://www.afro.com/archives/.

"Baltimore Afro-American—Google News Archive Search." Accessed 2 November 2019. https://news.google.com/newspapers/p/afro?nid=JkxM1axsR-IC&dat=19560303&printsec=frontpage&hl=en.

The New York Times. Accessed September 19, 2020. http://timesmachine.nytimes.com/timesmachine/1956/02/23/313801222.html.

Oral Interviews

Jeannie and Robert Graetz. Interview by author. Montgomery, Alabama. 14 June 2019.

Jo Ann Robinson. Interview by David Garrow. 5 April 1984. Transcript sent to author by David Garrow.

"Documenting the American South: Oral Histories of the American South." https://docsouth.unc.edu/sohp/U-0020/excerpts/excerpt_4851.html.

SECONDARY SOURCES

Anievas, Alexander, Nivi Manchanda, Robbie Shilliam, Nivi Manchanda, and Robbie Shilliam. *Race and Racism in International Relations: Confronting the Global Colour Line.* Routledge, 2014. https://doi.org/10.4324/9781315857299.

Aspinall, Peter J., and Martha J. Chinouya. "African Communities in Britain." In The African Diaspora Population in Britain: Migrant Identities and Experiences, edited by Peter J. Aspinall and Martha Judith Chinouya, 1–9. Migration, Diasporas and Citizenship. London: Palgrave Macmillan UK, 2016. https://doi.org/10.1057/978-1-137-45654-0_1.

Aydin, Andrew. "Cover Story: The Comic Book That Changed the World." Accessed 4 November 2019. https://creativeloafing.com/content-185638-cover-story-the-comic-book-that-changed-the.

———. "The Comic Book that Changed the World." Master's thesis. Georgetown University, 2012.

Azaransky, Sarah. *This Worldwide Struggle: Religion and the International Roots of the Civil Rights Movement.* Oxford University Press, 2017.

BBC. "Bristol's Black History Preserved." BBC. Accessed August 28, 2020. http://www.bbc.co.uk/bristol/content/articles/2007/08/31/bbap_feature.shtml.

"BBC - Gloucestershire Voices: Our Untold Stories - The Pakistani Community." Accessed September 23, 2020. http://www.bbc.co.uk/gloucestershire/untold_stories/asian/pakistani_community.shtml.

Beetham, David. *Transport and Turbans: A Comparative Study in Local Politics.* London, New York: Published for the Institute of Race Relations, London by Oxford U.P., 1970.

Blain, Keisha N. *Set the World on Fire: Black Nationalist Women and the Global Struggle for Freedom.* Philadelphia: University of Pennsylvania Press, 2018.

Blinder, Alan. "Bombed by the K.K.K. A Friend of Rosa Parks. At 90, This White Pastor Is Still Fighting." *The New York Times,* 17 August 2018, sec. U.S. https://www.nytimes.com/2018/08/17/us/rosa-parks-kkk-montgomery.html.

Borstelmann, Thomas. *The Cold War and the Color Line: American Race Relations in the Global Arena.* Cambridge, MA: Harvard University Press, c2001.

Branch, Taylor. *Parting the Waters: America in the King Years, 1954–1963.* New York: Simon and Schuster, c1988.

"Bristol and the Transatlantic Slave Trade." M Shed. Bristol, England.

"Bristol Population 2019 (Demographics, Maps, Graphs)." Accessed 17 September 2019. http://worldpopulationreview.com/world-cities/bristol-population/.

Brooks, Pamela E. *Boycotts, Buses, and Passes: Black Women's Resistance in the U.S. South and South Africa.* Amherst: University of Massachusetts Press, c2008.

Burns, Stewart. *Daybreak of Freedom [Electronic Resource]: The Montgomery Bus Boycott.* Chapel Hill, N.C.: University of North Carolina Press, 1997.

Camp, Stephanie M. H. *Closer to Freedom [Electronic Resource]: Enslaved Women and Everyday Resistance in the Plantation South.* Chapel Hill: University of North Carolina Press, c2004.

Carter, Bob, Marci Green, and Rick Halpern. "Immigration Policy and the Racialization of Migrant Labour: The Construction of National Identities in the USA and Britain." *Ethnic and Racial Studies* 19, no.

1 (1 January 1996): 135–57. https://doi.org/10.1080/01419870.19 96.9993902.

Carter, Bob, Clive Harris, and Shirley Joshi. "The 1951–55 Conservative Government and the Racialization of Black Immigration." *Immigrants & Minorities* 6, no. 3 (1987): 335–47. https://doi.org/10.1080/026 19288.1987.9974665.

Chabot, Sean. *Transnational Roots of the Civil Rights Movement: African American Explorations of the Gandhian Repertoire.* Lanham, Md.: Lexington Books, c2012.

"Claudia Jones and the 'West Indian Gazette' | Institute of Race Relations." Accessed 18 November 2019. http://www.irr.org.uk/news/claudia-jones-and-the-west-indian-gazette/.

Cobb, Charles E. *This Nonviolent Stuff'll Get You Killed: How Guns Made the Civil Rights Movement Possible.* New York, NY: Basic Books, a member of the Perseus Books Group, 2014.

Cone, James H. *A Black Theology of Liberation.* Maryknoll, N.Y.: Orbis Books, c1986.

Costello, Matthew J. (Matthew John). *Secret Identity Crisis [Electronic Resource]: Comic Books and the Unmasking of Cold War America.* New York: Continuum, c2009.

D'Emilio, John. *Lost Prophet: The Life and Times of Bayard Rustin.* New York: Free Press, c2003.

Dixie, Quinton Hosford. *Visions of a Better World: Howard Thurman's Pilgrimage to India and the Origins of African American Nonviolence.* Boston: Beacon Press, c2011.

Dresser, Madge. *Black and White On the Buses: The 1963 Colour Bar Dispute in Bristol.* Bristol Broadsides, 1986.

———. "Britain's History and Memory of Transatlantic Slavery: Local Nuances of a 'National Sin.'" *Social History* 42, no. 4 (2017): 555–556. https://doi.org/10.1080/03071022.2017.1359987.

———. "Remembering Slavery and Abolition in Bristol." *Slavery & Abolition* 30, no. 2 (1 June 2009): 223–46. https://doi.org/10.1080/01440390902818955.

Dudziak, Mary L. *Cold War Civil Rights: Race and the Image of American Democracy.* Princeton, N.J.: Princeton University Press, c2000.

Dummett, Michael. "Montgomery (and A. Cooke)." *Critical Philosophy of*

Race 3, no. 1 (2015): 1. https://doi.org/10.5325/critphilrace.3.1.0001.

Durr, Virginia Foster. *Outside the Magic Circle: The Autobiography of Virginia Foster Durr*. University, AL: University of Alabama Press, c1985.

Elphick, Richard. *The Equality of Believers [Electronic Resource]: Protestant Missionaries and the Racial Politics of South Africa*. Charlottesville: University of Virginia Press, 2012.

Equal Justice Initiative (EJI). "Slavery in America: the Montgomery Slave Trade." https://eji.org/reports/slavery-in-america/, https://museumand-memorial.eji.org/museum.

———. Legacy Museum. https://museumandmemorial.eji.org/museum

Fairclough, Adam. "Historians and the Civil Rights Movement." *Journal of American Studies* 24, no. 3 (1990): 387–98.

Foner, Nancy. "Gender and Migration: West Indians in Comparative Perspective." *International Migration* 47, no. 1 (2009): 3–29. https://doi.org/10.1111/j.1468-2435.2008.00480.x.

Francis, Elliott. "MLK Comic Book Helped Inspire Arab Spring." *WAMU* (blog). Accessed September 30, 2020. https://wamu.org/story/11/08/24/mlk_comic_book_helped_inspire_arab_spring/.

Frazier, Robeson Taj. *The East Is Black: Cold War China in the Black Radical Imagination*. Durham: Duke University Press, 2015.

Gaillard, Frye. *Cradle of Freedom: Alabama and the Movement That Changed America*. Tuscaloosa: University of Alabama Press, 2004.

Gandhi, Mohandas K. "An Autobiography: The Story of My Experiments with Truth," 1925; Ed. by Mahadev Desai, 1940." Accessed November 21, 2019. http://www.columbia.edu/itc/mealac/pritchett/00litlinks/gandhi/.

Garrow, David J. *Bearing the Cross: Martin Luther King, Jr., and the Southern Christian Leadership Conference*. New York: W. Morrow, c1986.

———ed. *The Walking City: The Montgomery Bus Boycott, 1955–1956*. Martin Luther King, Jr. and the Civil Rights Movement 7. Brooklyn, N.Y: Carlson Pub, 1989.

Gilroy, Paul. *The Black Atlantic: Modernity and Double Consciousness*. Cambridge, Mass: Harvard University Press, 1993.

Graetz, Robert S. *White Preacher's Memoir: The Montgomery Bus Boycott*. Montgomery: Black Belt Press, c1998.

Grant, Nicholas. *Winning Our Freedoms Together: African Americans and*

Apartheid, 1945–1960. Chapel Hill: University of North Carolina Press, 2017.

Gray, Fred D. *Bus Ride to Justice: Changing the System by the System: The Life and Works of Fred D. Gray, Preacher, Attorney, Politician.* Montgomery: NewSouth Books (1995), 2013.

Guild, Joshua Bruce. "You Can't Go Home Again: Migration, Citizenship, and Black Community in Postwar New York and London." Ph.D., Yale University, 2007.

Herbstein, Denis. "Obituary: Brian Bunting." *The Guardian*, 8 July 2008, sec. World news. https://www.theguardian.com/world/2008/jul/09/southafrica.pressandpublishing.

Higginbotham, Evelyn Brooks. *Righteous Discontent: The Women's Movement in the Black Baptist Church, 1880–1920.* Cambridge, Mass: Harvard University Press, 1993.

"History & Tradition | Alabama State University." Accessed May 14, 2020. https://www.alasu.edu/about-asu/history-tradition.

Howard, Sheena C., and Ronald L. Jackson, eds. *Black Comics: Politics of Race and Representation.* London; New York: Bloomsbury Academic, an imprint of Bloomsbury Publishing Plc, 2013.

Jackson, Thomas F. *From Civil Rights to Human Rights: Martin Luther King, Jr., and the Struggle for Economic Justice.* Philadelphia, Pa: University of Pennsylvania Press, c2007.

Jackson, Troy. *Becoming King: Martin Luther King, Jr. and the Making of a National Leader /.* Lexington, Ky.: University Press of Kentucky, c2008.

Juravich, Nick. "Your Fight is Our Fight: Transnationalism and the Development of Civil Rights Protest in Britain, 1960–1965." Master's thesis. University of Oxford, 2008.

Kamin, Ben. *Dangerous Friendship: Stanley Levison, Martin Luther King Jr., and the Kennedy Brothers.* East Lansing: Michigan State University Press, 2014.

Kapur, Sudarshan. *Raising up a Prophet: The African-American Encounter with Gandhi.* Boston: Beacon Press, c1992.

Katagiri, Yasuhiro. *Black Freedom, White Resistance, and Red Menace: Civil Rights and Anticommunism in the Jim Crow South.* Baton Rouge: Louisiana State University Press, 2014.

Kelley, Robin D. G. "'We Are Not What We Seem': Rethinking Black

Working-Class Opposition in the Jim Crow South." *The Journal of American History* 80, no. 1 (1993): 75–112.

Kelley, Robin D. G., and Stephen G. N. Tuck, eds. *The Other Special Relationship: Race, Rights, and Riots in Britain and the United States.* First edition. Contemporary Black History. New York, NY: Palgrave Macmillan, 2015.

Kelly, Jon. "What Was behind the Bristol Bus Boycott?" *BBC News*, 27 August 2013, sec. Magazine. https://www.bbc.com/news/magazine-23795655.

"Kelly on Letwin, 'The Challenge of Interracial Unionism: Alabama Coal Miners, 1878–1921' | H-Labor | H-Net." Accessed October 1, 2020. https://networks.h-net.org/node/7753/reviews/7963/kelly-letwin-challenge-interracial-unionism-alabama-coal-miners-1878.

Kosek, Joseph Kip. *Acts of Conscience [Electronic Resource]: Christian Nonviolence and Modern American Democracy.* New York: Columbia University Press, c2009.

Landau, Paul S. "The ANC, MK, and 'The Turn to Violence' (1960–1962)." *South African Historical Journal* 64, no. 3 (1 September 2012): 538–63. https://doi.org/10.1080/02582473.2012.660785.

Legacy Museum and National Memorial for Peace and Justice. "Legacy Museum: From Enslavement to Mass Incarceration." Accessed February 6, 2020. https://museumandmemorial.eji.org/museum.

Lepore, Jill. *The Secret History of Wonder Woman.* New York: Alfred A. Knopf, 2014.

Levine, Daniel. *Bayard Rustin and the Civil Rights Movement.* New Brunswick, N.J.: Rutgers University Press, 2000.

Lewis, Earl. "To Turn as on a Pivot: Writing African Americans into a History of Overlapping Diasporas." *The American Historical Review* 100, no. 3 (1995): 765–87. https://doi.org/10.2307/2168604.

Lewis, John. *Walking with the Wind: A Memoir of the Movement.* New York, NY: Simon & Schuster, 1998.

Malik, Kenan. "Racist Rhetoric Hasn't Been Consigned to Britain's Past | Kenan Malik." *The Guardian*, 4 March 2018, sec. Opinion. https://www.theguardian.com/commentisfree/2018/mar/04/commonwealth-immigrants-act-1968-racism.

Mansour, Claire. "The Cross-National Diffusion of the American Civil Rights Movement: The Example of the Bristol Bus Boycott of 1963."

MIRANDA, 2014. https://doi.org/10.4000/miranda.6360.

Masuoka, Jitsuichi. *Race Relations: Problems and Theory; Essays in Honor of Robert E. Park*. Chapel Hill: University of North Carolina Press, 1961.

Matera, Marc. *Black London: The Imperial Metropolis and Decolonization in the Twentieth Century*. Oakland, California: University of California Press, 2015.

Meier, August. *CORE; a Study in the Civil Rights Movement, 1942–1968*. New York: Oxford University Press, 1973.

"Milestones: 1945–1952 - Office of the Historian." Accessed 6 February 2020. https://history.state.gov/milestones/1945-1952/immigration-act.

Morgan, Iwan W., and Philip Davies, eds. *From Sit-Ins to SNCC: The Student Civil Rights Movement in the 1960s*. Gainesville: University Press of Florida, 2012.

Murphy, Alison L. "Fifty Years of Challenges to the Colorline Montgomery, Alabama." Thesis. Georgia State University, 2009. https://scholarworks.gsu.edu/history_theses/37

Nagler, Michael N. *Is There No Other Way?: The Search for a Nonviolent Future*. Berkeley, Calif: Berkeley Hills Books, c2001.

"Negro Leaders Arrested in Alabama Bus Boycott; 20 MINISTERS HELD IN NEGRO BOYCOTT Mass March Called." Accessed September 19, 2020. http://timesmachine.nytimes.com/timesmachine/1956/02/23/313801222.html.

Nesbitt, Francis Njubi. *Race for Sanctions: African Americans against Apartheid, 1946–1994*. Bloomington: Indiana University Press, 2004.

"NewSouth Books." Accessed September 14, 2020. http://www.newsouthbooks.com/pages/about/.

"No Moratorium on the Sermon on the Mount." Accessed September 13, 2020. http://deatspeace.tripod.com/muriel.html.

Olson, Lynne. *Freedom's Daughters: The Unsung Heroines of the Civil Rights Movement from 1830 to 1970*. New York: Scribner, c2001.

Pace, Eric. "Virginia F. Durr, 95, Advocate Of Civil Rights in the Deep South." *The New York Times*, February 26, 1999, sec. U.S. https://www.nytimes.com/1999/02/26/us/virginia-f-durr-95-advocate-of-civil-rights-in-the-deep-south.html.

Parks, Rosa. *Rosa Parks, My Story*. New York: Dial Books, c1992.

Peach, Ceri. *West Indian Migration to Britain: A Social Geography*. London: Oxford University Press for the Institute of Race Relations, 1968.

Pearson, David. *Race, Class and Political Activism: A Study of West Indians in Britain*. Farnborough, Hants: Gower, 1981.

Pennybacker, Susan D. (Susan Dabney). *From Scottsboro to Munich: Race and Political Culture in 1930s Britain*. Princeton, N.J.: Princeton University Press, c2009.

Perry, Kennetta Hammond. *London Is the Place for Me: Black Britons, Citizenship, and the Politics of Race*. New York, NY: Oxford University Press, 2015.

Phillips, Brian. "Making Necessary Trouble." *Journal of Human Rights Practice* 6, no. 2 (1 July 2014): 380–86. https://doi.org/10.1093/jhuman/huu007.

Pryce, Ken. *Endless Pressure: A Study of West Indian Life-Styles in Bristol*. 2d ed. Classical Press, Dept of Classics, University of Bristol, 1986.

Putnam, Lara. "The Transnational and the Text-Searchable: Digitized Sources and the Shadows They Cast." *American Historical Review* 121, no. 2 (April 2016). https://doi.org/10.1093/ahr/121.2.377.

———. *Radical Moves [Electronic Resource]: Caribbean Migrants and the Politics of Race in the Jazz Age*. Chapel Hill: University of North Carolina Press, c2013.

Reddick, Lawrence Dunbar. *Crusader without Violence: a Biography of Martin Luther King, Jr.* New York: Harper, 1959.

"Rep. John Lewis' Fight For Civil Rights Began With A Letter To Martin Luther King Jr." NPR.org. Accessed September 15, 2020. https://www.npr.org/2020/01/17/796954200/rep-john-lewis-fight-for-civil-rights-began-with-a-letter-to-martin-luther-king-.

Richardson, David and Bristol Record Society, eds., *Bristol, Africa, and the Eighteenth-Century Slave Trade to America*, Bristol Record Society's Publications, v. 38–39, 42, 47 (Gloucester: Produced for the Bristol Record Society by A. Sutton Pub, 1986).

Richmond, Anthony H. "Housing and Racial Attitudes in Bristol." *Race* 12, no. 1 (July 1970): 49–58. https://doi:10.1177/030639687001200103.

Roberts, Brian Russell, and Keith Foulcher, eds. *Indonesian Notebook: A Sourcebook on Richard Wright and the Bandung Conference*. Durham; London: Duke University Press, 2016.

Robertson, R. J. D. *The Small Beginning: The Story of North End Presbyterian Church, East London, 1962–1970*. Cape Town: s.n., 1997.

Robinson, Jo Ann Gibson. *The Montgomery Bus Boycott and the Women Who Started It: The Memoir of Jo Ann Gibson Robinson*. Knoxville: University of Tennessee Press, 1987.

Scalmer, Sean. *Gandhi in the West: The Mahatma and the Rise of Radical Protest*. Cambridge: Cambridge University Press, 2011.

Slate, Nico. *Colored Cosmopolitanism: The Shared Struggle for Freedom in the United States and India*. Cambridge, Mass: Harvard University Press, 2012.

Stanton, Mary. *Journey toward Justice: Juliette Hampton Morgan and the Montgomery Bus Boycott*. Athens: University of Georgia Press, c2006.

Stephenson, Paul and Lileith Morrison. *Memoirs of a Black Englishman*. Bristol: Tangent Books, 2011.

"Sweet Auburn Historic District—Atlanta: A National Register of Historic Places Travel Itinerary." Accessed November 30, 2019. https://www.nps.gov/nr/travel/atlanta/aub.htm.

"South Asians in Bristol | Historians at Bristol." Accessed September 2, 2020. https://historiansatbristol.blogs.bristol.ac.uk/archives/tag/south-asians-in-bristol.

Terry, Bryan. "Towards 'The World House': Dr. Martin Luther King, Jr.'s Global Vision of Peace and Justice, 1956–1968." *History Theses*, December 17, 2014. https://scholarworks.gsu.edu/history_theses/87.

"The Afro-American." Accessed November 9, 2019. https://www.pbs.org/blackpress/news_bios/afroamerican.html.

"The Bristol Bus Boycott 1963." Plaque. Bristol bus station, United Kingdom. Photo by author.

"The Joseph Rowntree Charitable Trust." Accessed February 9, 2020. https://www.jrct.org.uk/.

"The National Archives | Brave New World." Accessed April 9, 2020. http://www.nationalarchives.gov.uk/pathways/citizenship/brave_new_world/immigration.htm.

———. "Commonwealth Immigration Control and Legislation." Accessed February 9, 2020. https://www.nationalarchives.gov.uk/cabinetpapers/themes/commonwealth-immigration-control-legislation.htm.

Theoharis, Jeanne. *The Rebellious Life of Mrs. Rosa Parks*. Boston: Beacon

Press, c2013.

The Martin Luther King, Jr., Research and Education Institute, April 24, 2017. https://kinginstitute.stanford.edu/encyclopedia/ballou-maude-l-williams.

———. "Browder v. Gayle, 352 U.S. 903," April 24, 2017, https://kinginstitute.stanford.edu/encyclopedia/browder-v-gayle-352-us-903.

———. "Ghana Trip." April 26, 2017. https://kinginstitute.stanford.edu/encyclopedia/ghana-trip.

———. "India Trip." June 20, 2017. https://kinginstitute.stanford.edu/encyclopedia/india-trip.

———. "Robinson, Jo Ann Gibson." June 22, 2017. https://kinginstitute.stanford.edu/encyclopedia/robinson-jo-ann-gibson.

Thornton, J. Mills, III. "Challenge and Response in the Montgomery Bus Boycott of 1955–1956." *Alabama Review* 67, no. 1 (January 2014): 40–112. https://doi.org/10.1353/ala.2014.0000.

Turnbull, Thomas. "Themes of the 1963 Bristol Bus Boycott." Master's thesis. Newcastle University, 2015.

Von Eschen, Penny M. (Penny Marie). *Race against Empire: Black Americans and Anticolonialism, 1937–1957*. Ithaca, NY: Cornell University Press, 1997.

Wall, Tom. "Bristol's Walls of Fame Celebrate Seven 'Saints' Who Fought for Race Equality." *The Observer*, August 26, 2018, sec. UK news. https://www.theguardian.com/uk-news/2018/aug/26/bristol-wall-of-fame-st-pauls-seven-saints-of-carnival-race-equality.

Ward, Brian and Anthony Badger, eds. *The Making of Martin Luther King and the Civil Rights Movement*. Palgrave Macmillan UK, 1996.

Weber, Thomas. "The Impact of Gandhi on the Development of Johan Galtung's Peace Research." *Global Change, Peace & Security* 16, no. 1 (February 1, 2004): 31–43. https://doi.org/10.1080/1478115042000176166.

Westhauser, Karl E., Elaine M. Smith, and Jennifer A. Fremlin. *Creating Community: Life and Learning at Montgomery's Black University*. University of Alabama Press, 2005.

Wild, Rosalind Eleanor. "Black Was the Colour of Our Fight. Black Power in Britain, 1955–1976." http://etheses.whiterose.ac.uk/3640/.

Wilkerson, Isabel. *Caste: The Origins of Our Discontents*. New York:

Random House, 2020.

Williams, Eric Eustace. *Capitalism & Slavery*. Chapel Hill: University of North Carolina Press, 1994.

Woods, Jeff. *Black Struggle, Red Scare: Segregation and Anti-Communism in the South, 1948–1968*. Baton Rouge: Louisiana State University Press, c2003.

Woodward, C. Vann (Comer Vann). *Origins of the New South, 1877–1913 [Electronic Resource]*. Baton Rouge: Louisiana State University Press, 1971.

Wong, Josiah. "Why the Bus Station Has Been Named Top Place of UK Historical Importance." bristolpost, 6 August 2018. https://www.bristolpost.co.uk/news/bristol-news/bristol-bus-station-just-been-1867725.

York, Chris, and Rafiel York, eds. *Comic Books and the Cold War, 1946–1962: Essays on Graphic Treatment of Communism, the Code and Social Concerns*. Jefferson, N.C: McFarland, 2012.

Notes

1   "John Robert Lewis, SNCC Founder and Chairman, Civil Rights Leader, and Congressman, Dies at 80," The Martin Luther King, Jr., Research and Education Institute, July 20, 2020.

2   "Rep. John Lewis' Fight for Civil Rights Began with a Letter to Martin Luther King Jr.," NPR, January 17, 2020. See also: John Lewis, *Walking with the Wind: A Memoir of the Movement* (New York, NY: Simon & Schuster, 1998), 412.

3   Lara Putnam, "The Transnational and the Text-Searchable: Digitized Sources and the Shadows They Cast," *The American Historical Review* 121, no. 2 (April 2016), 377–402.

4   See: C. Vann (Comer Vann) Woodward, *Origins of the New South, 1877–1913 [Electronic Resource]* (Baton Rouge: Louisiana State University Press, 1971).

5   See: Robin D. G. Kelley and Stephen G. N. Tuck, eds., *The Other Special Relationship: Race, Rights, and Riots in Britain and the United States,* (New York, NY: Palgrave Macmillan, 2015).

6   See: Francis Njubi Nesbitt, *Race for Sanctions: African Americans against Apartheid, 1946–1994* (Bloomington: Indiana University Press, 2004); Nicholas Grant, *Winning Our Freedoms Together: African Americans and Apartheid, 1945–1960* (Chapel Hill: University of North Carolina Press, 2017).

7   Nick Juravich makes a similar point in his article. See: Kelley and Tuck, 83.

8   Tamara Ikenberg, "Publishing with a Purpose," *The Courier Journal*, February 19 2008, http://www.newsouthbooks.com/pages/wp-content/uploads/2008/03/nsb-cj-article.pdf.

9   Martin Luther King Institute, "Robinson, Jo Ann Gibson," 22 June 2017, https://kinginstitute.stanford.edu/encyclopedia/robinson-jo-ann-gibson.

10 ARC, Preston and Bonita Valien Papers, Series 2: Southern desegregation field reports and notes, 1941-1961, Box 2.

11 ARC, Valien Papers, Series 2, Box 2, 26 March 1956 "Mass Meeting, Montgomery Improvement Association."

12 Sarah Azaransky, *This Worldwide Struggle,* (Oxford: Oxford University Press, 2017).

13 Isabel Wilkerson's *Caste* is a recent addition to scholarship that explores connections between freedom struggles and white supremacy in India and in the

United States. See: Isabel Wilkerson, *Caste: The Origins of Our Discontents* (New York: Random House, 2020).

14 SC, George R. Metcalf Papers, Box 1, Folder 1, "Martin Luther King, Jr."

15 Stewart Burns, *Daybreak of Freedom: The Montgomery Bus Boycott* (Chapel Hill, N.C.: University of North Carolina Press, 1997), 23.

16 Robin D. G. Kelley, "'We Are Not What We Seem': Rethinking Black Working-Class Opposition in the Jim Crow South." *The Journal of American History* 80, no. 1 (1993): 78.

17 On Bandung, see: Brian Russell Roberts and Keith Foulcher, eds., *Indonesian Notebook: A Sourcebook on Richard Wright and the Bandung Conference* (Durham; London: Duke University Press, 2016).

18 "Ghana Trip," 26 April 2017, https://kinginstitute.stanford.edu/encyclopedia/ghana-trip.

19 "India Trip," 20 June 2017, https://kinginstitute.stanford.edu/encyclopedia/india-trip.

20 David J. Garrow, *Bearing the Cross: Martin Luther King, Jr., and the Southern Christian Leadership Conference* (New York: W. Morrow, c1986).

21 Taylor Branch, *Parting the Waters: America in the King Years, 1954-1963* (New York: Simon and Schuster, c1988).

22 Jeanne Theoharis' work on Rosa Parks explores how her long history of organizing was de-emphasized and ignored by both movement colleagues and by historians writing years later. See: Jeanne Theoharis, *The Rebellious Life of Mrs. Rosa Parks* (Boston: Beacon Press, c2013).

23 See: Thomas Borstelmann, *The Cold War and the Color Line: American Race Relations in the Global Arena* (Cambridge, MA: Harvard University Press, c2001); Mary L. Dudziak, *Cold War Civil Rights: Race and the Image of American Democracy* (Princeton, N.J.: Princeton University Press, c2000).

24 See: Jo Ann Gibson Robinson, *Montgomery Bus Boycott and the Women Who Started It: The Memoir of Jo Ann Gibson Robinson* (Knoxville: University of Tennessee Press, 1987).

25 See: Rosa Parks, *Rosa Parks, My Story* (New York: Dial Books, c1992.); Virginia Foster Durr, *Outside the Magic Circle: The Autobiography of Virginia Foster Durr* (University, AL: University of Alabama Press, c1985).

26 See: Kennetta Hammond Perry, *London Is the Place for Me: Black Britons, Citizenship, and the Politics of Race* (New York, NY: Oxford University Press, 2015); Marc Matera, *Black London: The Imperial Metropolis and Decolonization in the Twentieth Century* (Oakland, California: University of California Press, 2015); Susan Pennybacker, *From Scottsboro to Munich: Race and Political Culture in 1930s Britain* (Princeton, N.J.: Princeton University Press, c2009).

27 Earl Lewis, "To Turn as on a Pivot: Writing African Americans into a History of Overlapping Diasporas," *The American Historical Review* 100, no. 3 (1995): 765–87, https://doi.org/10.2307/2168604.

28 Martin Luther King Jr. Institute, "Montgomery City Officials Reject MIA Proposals; King Consults T. J. Jemison; MIA Approves Car Pool," The Martin Luther King, Jr., Research and Education Institute, June 22, 2017, https:// kinginstitute.stanford.edu/encyclopedia/montgomery-city-officials-reject-mia-proposals-king-consults-t-j-jemison-mia-approves.

29 ARC, Preston and Bonita Valien Papers, Box 1, Field Notes by Dr. Inez Adams, January 24 and 26, 1956.

30 ARC, Valien Papers, Box 2, January 20, 1956 interview of Rufus A. Lewis, by Donald Ferron, 2–3.

31 ARC, Valien Papers, Box 2, January 27, 1956 interview of Rev. Wilson by Donald Ferron.

32 ARC, Valien Papers, Box 2, January 27, 1956 interview of Rev. Wilson by Donald Ferron.

33 ADAH, Virginia Durr Papers, Patricia Sullivan, *Freedom Writer,* March 24, 1956 Letter.

34 Eric Pace, "Virginia F. Durr, 95, Advocate Of Civil Rights in the Deep South," *The New York Times,* February 26, 1999, sec. U.S., https://www.nytimes.com/1999/02/26/us/virginia-f-durr-95-advocate-of-civil-rights-in-the-deep-south.html.

35 ADAH, Virginia Durr Papers, Patricia Sullivan, *Freedom Writer,* February-March 1956 Letter.

36 ADAH, Lyon Addition to Durr Papers, Box 3, Folder 7, Jack Rabin Interview with Clifford and Virginia Durr July 6, 1974, by Dr. Jack Rabin and Mr. Daniel Crapps.

37 Martin Luther King Jr. Institute, "Montgomery Bus Boycott," The Martin Luther King, Jr., Research and Education Institute, April 26, 2017, https:// kinginstitute.stanford.edu/encyclopedia/montgomery-bus-boycott. See also Fred D. Gray, *Bus Ride to Justice: Changing the System by the System* (Montgomery: NewSouth Books, 2013), 84.

38 "Kelly on Letwin, 'The Challenge of Interracial Unionism: Alabama Coal Miners, 1878–1921' | H-Labor | H-Net," accessed October 1, 2020, https://networks.h-net.org/node/7753/reviews/7963/ kelly-letwin-challenge-interracial-unionism-alabama-coal-miners-1878.

39 ARC, Valien Papers, Box 2, March 1, 1956, Mass Meeting at Holt Street Baptist Church.

40 Martin Luther King Jr. Institute, "State of Alabama v. M. L. King, Jr., Nos. 7399 and 9593," The Martin Luther King, Jr., Research and Education

Institute, July 7, 2017, https://kinginstitute.stanford.edu/encyclopedia/ state-alabama-v-m-l-king-jr-nos-7399-and-9593.

41 "Negro Leaders Arrested in Alabama Bus Boycott; 20 MINISTERS HELD IN NEGRO BOYCOTT Mass March Called," accessed September 19, 2020, http://timesmachine.nytimes.com/timesmachine/1956/02/23/313801222. html.

42 ARC, Valien Papers, Box 3, February 28, 1956 letter to Dr. Valien from J. Harold Jones.

43 "King's Home Bombed," https://kinginstitute.stanford.edu/encyclopedia/ kings-home-bombed.

44 Nico Slate, *Colored Cosmopolitanism: The Shared Struggle for Freedom in the United States and India* (Cambridge: Harvard University Press, 2012), 221.

45 ASU, Montgomery Bus Boycott Newspaper Clippings Collection, 1955– 1956, December 12, 1955, editorial *Montgomery Advertiser.*

46 Jeannie and Robert Graetz, Interview by author, Montgomery, Alabama, June 14, 2019.

47 Alan Blinder, "Bombed by the K.K.K. A Friend of Rosa Parks. At 90, This White Pastor Is Still Fighting.," *The New York Times,* 17 August 2018, sec. U.S., https://www.nytimes.com/2018/08/17/us/rosa-parks-kkk-montgomery. html.

48 ASU, December 12, 1955, editorial.

49 Mary Stanton, *Journey toward Justice: Juliette Hampton Morgan and the Montgomery Bus Boycott* (Athens: University of Georgia Press, 2006).

50 Clayborne Carson, Stewart Burns, Susan Carson, Dana Powell, and Peter Holloran, eds., *The Papers of Martin Luther King, Jr.* Volume III: Birth of a New Age, December 1955–December 1956, (Berkeley: University of California Press, 1997), 138.

51 Ibid., 19.

52 Ibid., 20.

53 SCPC, Fellowship of Reconciliation Records, DG 013, Series D: Rustin and Smiley Staff Papers, Box 51, FOR Program Staff: Bayard Rustin.

54 *Papers,* 20.

55 On the presence of guns in civil rights struggles, see: Charles E. Cobb, *This Nonviolent Stuff'll Get You Killed: How Guns Made the Civil Rights Movement Possible* (New York, NY: Basic Books, a member of the Perseus Books Group, 2014).

56 Jeanne Theoharis, *The Rebellious Life of Mrs. Rosa Parks* (Boston: Beacon Press, 2013), 67.

57 *Rosa Parks,* 105.

58 Theoharis, 40.

59 Kapur, 151.

60 Theoharis, 64.

61 For more on Parks: "Documenting the American South: Oral Histories of the American South."

62 SCPC, John Nevin Sayre Papers, DG 117, Series I.

63 SCPC, Sayre Papers, DG 117, Series B: International Files, 1922–1974, Box 22, International Correspondence, Great Britain, April 19, 1956, Letter to Vera Brittain.

64 SCPC, Sayre Papers, DG 117, Series I.

65 Kapur, 87.

66 SCPC, Sayre Papers, DG 117, Series B: International Files, Box 26, June 19, 1956, Letter to Muriel Lester.

67 *Papers,* 183.

68 Nico Slate, *Colored Cosmopolitanism: The Shared Struggle for Freedom in the United States and India* (Cambridge, Mass: Harvard University Press, 2012), 222.

69 *Papers*, 21.

70 Ibid.

71 James H. Cone, *A Black Theology of Liberation* (Maryknoll, N.Y.: Orbis Books, 1986), 23.

72 "The Weaknesses of Liberal Theology," The Martin Luther King, Jr., Research and Education Institute, October 11, 2016.

73 Slate, 222.

74 Thomas F. Jackson, *From Civil Rights to Human Rights: Martin Luther King, Jr., and the Struggle for Economic Justice* (Philadelphia, Pa: University of Pennsylvania Press, 2007), 69.

75 "King's World House," The Martin Luther King, Jr., Research and Education Institute, February 20, 2019.

76 "Sweet Auburn Historic District—Atlanta: A National Register of Historic Places Travel Itinerary," Accessed November 30, 2019.

77 "An Autobiography of Religious Development," The Martin Luther King, Jr., Research and Education Institute.

78 Ibid.

79 Jackson, 26.

80 Ibid., 33.

81 Ibid., 34–35.

82 Jo Ann Gibson Robinson, *Montgomery Bus Boycott and the Women Who*

Started It: The Memoir of Jo Ann Gibson Robinson (Knoxville: University of Tennessee Press, 1987), xii, 9–10.

83 Lynne Olson, *Freedom's Daughters: The Unsung Heroines of the Civil Rights Movement from 1830 to 1970* (New York: Scribner, 2001), 91.

84 J. Mills Thornton III, "Challenge and Response in the Montgomery Bus Boycott of 1955–1956," *Alabama Review* 67, no. 1 (January 2014): 40–112.

85 Jo Ann Robinson, The Martin Luther King, Jr., Research and Education Institute.

86 Robinson, "Don't Ride the Bus," The Martin Luther King, Jr., Research and Education Institute, December 2, 1955.

87 Robinson, *Women Who Started It,* 15–16.

88 Garrow, *Bearing the Cross,* 14.

89 *Women Who Started It,* x.

90 Kelley, "We Are Not What We Seem," 102.

91 Kelley, 105.

92 Kelley, 105.

93 ARC, Valien Papers, Series 2, Box 2, January 20, 1956, interview of Rufus Lewis by Donald Ferron, 6.

94 ARC, January 20, 1956 interview, 6.

95 Jo Ann Robinson, interview by David Garrow, April 5, 1984, transcript sent to author by David Garrow.

96 Burns, 4.

97 SCPC, FOR Records, Series E: Bus Boycott Program Materials, Box 18, Race Relations, MIA newsletters, Volume 1, No 1, June 7, 1956, 3.

98 SCPC, FOR Records, Series E, Box 18, MIA newsletters, Volume 1, No 1, June 7, 1956, 3.

99 "Agape," The Martin Luther King, Jr., Research and Education Institute, April 24, 2017.

100 "History & Tradition | Alabama State University," accessed May 14, 2020, https://www.alasu.edu/about-asu/history-tradition.

101 ASU, Montgomery Bus Boycott Newspaper Clippings Collection, February 2, 1956, *Atlanta Daily World*, "Dr. Reddick Analyzes Ala. Bus Situation," William Gordon, 1.

102 Ibid.

103 ARC, Valien Papers, Box 2, February 1, 1956 interview of Mr. Prince Conley by Ferron.

104 ADAH, James Folsom papers, Administrative Files, Segregation, April 1, 1956, to September 30, 1957, Folder 11, 23 February 1956 letter from Alice

Cole to Folsom.

105 Ibid., February 27, 1956, letter from J. Welch.

106 Jill Lepore, *The Secret History of Wonder Woman* (New York: Alfred A. Knopf, 2014), 179.

107 Andrew Aydin, "The Comic Book that Changed the World," Master's thesis, (Georgetown University, 2012), 17.

108 Aydin, 30. See: Matthew J. (Matthew John) Costello, *Secret Identity Crisis [Electronic Resource]: Comic Books and the Unmasking of Cold War America* (New York: Continuum, c2009), 7.

109 Chris York and Rafiel York, eds., *Comic Books and the Cold War, 1946–1962: Essays on Graphic Treatment of Communism, the Code and Social Concerns* (Jefferson, N.C: McFarland, 2012), 5.

110 York, 31.

111 Sheena C. Howard and Ronald L. Jackson, eds., *Black Comics: Politics of Race and Representation* (London; New York: Bloomsbury Academic, an imprint of Bloomsbury Publishing Plc, 2013), 2.

112 *Black Comics,* 51.

113 SCPC, FOR Records, Series E, Box 19: Race Relations, February 24, 1958, letter from J. Harold Sherk to Al Hassler.

114 SCPC, FOR Records, Series E, Box 19 Race Relations, Letter from Alfred Hassler to Edward Reed.

115 "No Moratorium on the Sermon on the Mount," accessed September 13, 2020, http://deatspeace.tripod.com/muriel.html.

116 Richard Deats, http://deatspeace.tripod.com/.

117 SCPC, FOR Records, Series E, Box 19 Race Relations, Letter from Richard Deats to Paul Gravett, April 30, 1997.

118 SCPC, FOR Records, *Martin Luther King and the Montgomery Story.*

119 Mohandas Gandhi, "An Autobiography: The Story of My Experiments with Truth, 1925; Ed. by Mahadev Desai, 1940," accessed September 7, 2020. http://www.columbia.edu/itc/mealac/pritchett/00litlinks/gandhi/.

120 Alexander Anievas et al., *Race and Racism in International Relations: Confronting the Global Colour Line* (Routledge, 2014), https://doi.org/10.4324/9781315857299, 145.

121 Ibid., 142–143.

122 See: Alexander Anievas et al., Race and Racism in International Relations : Confronting the Global Colour Line (Routledge, 2014), https://doi.org/10.4324/9781315857299.

123 See: Gandhi, Mohandas K. "An Autobiography: The Story of My Experiments with Truth," 1925; Ed. by Mahadev Desai, 1940." Accessed November 21,

2019. http://www.columbia.edu/itc/mealac/pritchett/00litlinks/gandhi/.

124 See: Michael N. Nagler, *Is There No Other Way? The Search for a Nonviolent Future* (Berkeley, Calif: Berkeley Hills Books, 2001).

125 SCPC, FOR Records, Series E, Box 19, April 30, 1997. Letter from Richard Deats to Paul Gravett.

126 SCPC, FOR Records, Series E, Box 19, 30 December 1957 Letter from Hugh Brock to Alfred Hassler.

127 Aydin, "Cover Story."

128 Denis Herbstein, "Obituary: Brian Bunting," *The Guardian*, 8 July 2008, sec. World news, https://www.theguardian.com/world/2008/jul/09/southafrica.pressandpublishing.

129 SCPC, FOR Records, Series E, Box 19, December 6, 1958. Letter from Brian Bunting to New York FOR.

130 Nicholas Grant cites a figure of 70,000 participants. See: Nicholas Grant, *Winning Our Freedoms Together: African Americans and Apartheid, 1945–1960* (Chapel Hill: University of North Carolina Press, 2017), 3.

131 Pamela E. Brooks, *Boycotts, Buses, and Passes: Black Women's Resistance in the U.S. South and South Africa* (Amherst: University of Massachusetts Press, 2008.), 163–164.

132 Ibid., 224.

133 Ibid., 230.

134 Ibid., 229.

135 SCPC, December 6, 1958, Letter.

136 Richard Elphick, *The Equality of Believers [Electronic Resource]: Protestant Missionaries and the Racial Politics of South Africa* (Charlottesville: University of Virginia Press, 2012), 134–135.

137 Elphick, 132.

138 Elphick, 319–320.

139 Elphick, 320.

140 Brian Phillips, "Making Necessary Trouble," Journal of Human Rights Practice 6, no. 2 (July 1, 2014): 380–86, https://doi.org/10.1093/jhuman/huu007.

141 SCPC, FOR Records, Series E, Box 19, July 27, 1959, Letter from Jerome Nkosi to New York FOR.

142 ADAH, Lyon Addition, Box 4, Folder 9, "Virginia Durr Interviews for Eyes on the Prize 1979–1986."

143 Ibid.

144 Grant, 7–8.

145 Grant, 8.

146 SCPC, FOR Records, Series B, Box 22, 28 May 1956 Letter from Brittain to Sayre.

147 ARC, Valien Papers, Box 2, 26 March 1956 "Mass Meeting, Montgomery Improvement Association."

148 EJI, "Slavery in America: the Montgomery Slave Trade," https://eji.org/reports/slavery-in-america/, https://museumandmemorial.eji.org/museum, 34.

149 EJI, "Legacy Museum," https://museumandmemorial.eji.org/museum.

150 Eric Eustace Williams, *Capitalism & Slavery* (Chapel Hill: University of North Carolina Press, 1994), 10, 15, 19.

151 Madge Dresser, "Remembering Slavery and Abolition in Bristol," *Slavery & Abolition 30*, no. 2 (1 June 2009): 223–46.

152 David Richardson and Bristol Record Society, eds., *Bristol, Africa, and the Eighteenth-Century Slave Trade to America*, Bristol Record Society's Publications, v. 38–39, 42, 47 (Gloucester: Produced for the Bristol Record Society by A. Sutton Pub, 1986), xvi.

153 Richardson, xxvi.

154 "Bristol and the Transatlantic Slave Trade," M Shed, Bristol, England.

155 Edward Pattillo, *Carolina Planters on the Alabama Frontier: The Spencer-Robeson-McKenzie Family Papers* (Montgomery: NewSouth Books, 2011).

156 Alison L Murphy, "Fifty Years of Challenges to the Colorline Montgomery, Alabama," Georgia State University, 1.

157 I refer to Afro-Caribbeans as "West Indians," as this is how they would have referred to themselves at the time. Population for Bristol in 1960, World Population Review.

158 "South Asians in Bristol | Historians at Bristol," https://historiansatbristol.blogs.bristol.ac.uk/archives/tag/south-asians-in-bristol.

159 "BBC— Gloucestershire Voices: Our Untold Stories —The Pakistani Community," accessed September 23, 2020.

160 Peter J. Aspinall and Martha J. Chinouya, "African Communities in Britain," in *The African Diaspora Population in Britain: Migrant Identities and Experiences*, ed. Peter J. Aspinall and Martha Judith Chinouya, Migration, Diasporas and Citizenship (London: Palgrave Macmillan UK, 2016), 1–9.

161 Ken Pryce, *Endless Pressure: A Study of West Indian Life-Styles in Bristol*, 2d ed, (Bristol: Classical Press, Dept of Classics, University of Bristol, 1986).

162 "Milestones: 1945–1952 - Office of the Historian."

163 Paul Stephenson OBE and Lileith Morrison, *Memoirs of a Black Englishman* (Bristol: Tangent Books, 2011), 16.

164 "The National Archives, Brave New World." See also: Ceri Peach, *West Indian Migration to Britain: A Social Geography* (London: Oxford University Press for the Institute of Race Relations, 1968).

165 Stephenson, 16. See also: Bob Carter, Marci Green, and Rick Halpern, "Immigration Policy and the Racialization of Migrant Labour: The Construction of National Identities in the USA and Britain."

166 Bob Carter, Clive Harris, and Shirley Joshi, "The 1951–55 Conservative Government And The Racialisation of Black Immigration," https://web.warwick.ac.uk/fac/soc/CRER_RC/publications/pdfs/Policy%20Papers%20in%20Ethnic%20Relations/PolicyP%20No.11.pdf, 2.

167 BA, Lurel Roy Hackett Files, Folder 2: Newspaper Cuttings, July 23, 2005, article in *Bristol Evening Post* by Sarah Feeley, "How Roy put down roots for his people."

168 Ibid.

169 Ibid., 14.

170 Ibid., 16.

171 IRR Newsletter, June 1963, *Western Daily Press*, May 4, 1963, 1.

172 IRR Newsletter, July 1963, "Bristol, After the Bus Dispute," by Peter Searle, 14.

173 Anthony H. Richmond, "Housing and Racial Attitudes in Bristol," *Race* 12, no. 1 (July 1970): 49–58, doi:10.1177/030639687001200103.

174 IRR Newsletter, "Bristol, After the Bus Dispute."

175 Dresser, *Black and White On the Buses: The 1963 Colour Bar Dispute in Bristol,* (Bristol: Bristol Broadsides, 1986), 14.

176 Nancy Foner, "Gender and Migration," 7.

177

178 Ceri Peach, *West Indian Migration to Britain: A Social Geography* (London: Oxford University Press for the Institute of Race Relations, 1968).

179 BA, Paul Stephenson Collection, 42840, Press Cuttings, 1963–2013, Printed Materials, Folder 1, 1962 article, "Jamboree Opening to Go Ahead," 1.

180 Dresser, 15.

181 Ibid.

182 "The Joseph Rowntree Charitable Trust," https://www.jrct.org.uk/.

183 Stephenson, 44.

184 Nick Juravich, "Your Fight is Our Fight: Transnationalism and the Development of Civil Rights Protest in Britain, 1960–1965," Master's thesis, University of Oxford, 82–83.

185 IRR, *West Indian Gazette,* December 1961, Vol. 4, No. 12.

186 The National Archives, "Commonwealth Immigration Control and Legislation."

187 IRR, *West Indian Gazette,* November 1961, Vol. 4, No. 11, October 13, 1961, editorial *Daily Gleaner.*

188 Juravich, 83. See also: Robin D. G. Kelley and Stephen G. N. Tuck, eds., *The Other Special Relationship: Race, Rights, and Riots in Britain and the United States,* (New York, NY: Palgrave Macmillan, 2015).

189 Stephen Tuck, "From Greensboro to Notting Hill: The Sit-Ins in England," in Iwan W. Morgan and Philip Davies, eds., *From Sit-Ins to SNCC: The Student Civil Rights Movement in the 1960s* (Gainesville: University Press of Florida, 2012), 153–154.

190 Perry, 10–11.

191 Mike Sewell, "British Responses to Martin Luther King and the Civil Rights Movement 1954–68," in Brian Ward and Anthony Badger, eds., *The Making of Martin Luther King and the Civil Rights Movement* (Palgrave Macmillan UK, 1996), 194.

192 IRR, *West Indian Gazette,* June 1963, Vol. 5, No. 11.

193 Claire Mansour, "The Cross—National Diffusion of the American Civil Rights Movement: The Example of the Bristol Bus Boycott of 1963," *MIRANDA,* 2014, https://doi.org/10.4000/miranda.6360.

194 BA, Filmed Interview.

195 Ibid.

196 Jon Kelly, "What Was behind the Bristol Bus Boycott?," *BBC News,* August 27, 2013, sec. Magazine.

197 Dresser, 15.

198 BA, Paul Stephenson Collection, 42840, Press Cuttings, 1963–2013, Printed Materials, Folder 3, *The Herald* May 1963, "Boycott on 'colour bar' buses."

199 Dresser, 17.

200 Jon Kelly, "What Was behind the Bristol Bus Boycott?"

201 Dresser, 17.

202 Stephanie M. H. Camp, *Closer to Freedom [Electronic Resource]: Enslaved Women and Everyday Resistance in the Plantation South* (Chapel Hill: University of North Carolina Press, c2004), 7.

203 BA, Paul Stephenson Collection, Press Cuttings, Printed Materials, Folder 3, *Bristol Evening Post* April 30, 1963, editorial, "Comment: Colour bar on Bristol buses."

204 Dresser, 22.

205 BA, Paul Stephenson Collection, Press Cuttings, Folder 3, April 30, 1963, unknown newspaper, "W. Indians 100 p.c. for bus boycott."

206 IRR Newsletter, June 1963.

207 Ibid.

208 July 23, 2005, article, "How Roy put down roots for his people."

209 BA, Paul Stephenson Collection, Folder 3, *Bristol Evening Post,* May 2, 1963, "Busmen heckle marchers."

210 Ibid."

211 Ibid.

212 BA, Paul Stephenson Collection, Press Cuttings, Folder 3, 1963 article, "Bristolian Writes from Jamaica."

213 "Gray, Fred David, Sr.," The Martin Luther King, Jr., Research and Education Institute, May 8, 2017.

214 TU, Southern School News, April 1956 Edition, "Citizens Councils See Biggest Membership Gain in Alabama," 5.

215 "Browder v. Gayle, 352 U.S. 903," The Martin Luther King, Jr., Research and Education Institute, April 24, 2017.

216 Thomas Turnbull, "Themes of the 1963 Bristol Bus Boycott," Master's thesis, Newcastle University, 2015, 34.

217 Ibid., 35.

218 "Transport Holding Company Bill - Hansard," https://hansard.parliament.uk/commons/1968-01-16/debates/eb0a4b40-d737-432d-b8b5-8c472e16f863/TransportHoldingCompanyBill.

219 IRR Newsletter, June 1963.

220 Ibid.

221 Evelyn Brooks Higginbotham, *Righteous Discontent: The Women's Movement in the Black Baptist Church, 1880–1920* (Cambridge: Harvard University Press, 1993), 187.

222 IRR Newsletter, June 1963.

223 Rosalind Eleanor Wild, "Black Was the Colour of Our Fight. Black Power in Britain, 1955–1976."

224 IRR Newsletter, June 1963.

225 Wild, 57.

226 BA, Paul Stephenson Collection, Filmed interview, 2009.

227 BA, Paul Stephenson Collection, Press Cuttings, Folder 3, August 28, 1963, article, by Pat Ravanagh, 1.

228 BA, Paul Stephenson Collection, Press Cuttings, Folder 3, *Daily Telegraph,* August 30, 1963, "Coloured Bus Crews Agreed: Bristol settlement over conductors."

229 Ibid.

230 Jon Kelly.

231 BA, Paul Stephenson Collection, Press Cuttings, Folder 3, 1963, unnamed newspaper, "End of Bus Colour Bar."

232 Dresser, 50.

233 Dresser, 57.

234 Kenan Malik, "Racist Rhetoric Hasn't Been Consigned to Britain's Past," *The Guardian*, March 4, 2018, sec. Opinion.

235 BA, Lurel Roy Hackett Files, Folder 2: Newspaper Cuttings, *The Jamaican Weekly Gleaner*, October 21, 1964: "Anti-segregationist comes to study Jamaicans' economic, social conditions."

236 ADAH, Virginia Durr Papers, Series II: Correspondence and Letters, Box 3, Folder 1, "Harkness Fellows, 1961–1974."

237 Karl E. Westhauser, Elaine M. Smith, and Jennifer A. Fremlin, *Creating Community: Life and Learning at Montgomery's Black University* (University of Alabama Press, 2005), 10.

238 Martin Luther King Jr. Institute, Jo Ann Robinson.

239 Martin Luther King Jr. Institute, Rosa Parks, https://kinginstitute.stanford.edu/encyclopedia/parks-rosa.

240 Juravich, 49–50.

241 BBC, "Bristol's Black History Preserved" (BBC), accessed August 28, 2020, http://www.bbc.co.uk/bristol/content/articles/2007/08/31/bbap_feature.shtml.

242 BBC, "Bristol's Black History Preserved."

243 BBC, "Bristol's Black History Preserved."

244 On the memory of slavery in the United Kingdom, see: Madge Dresser, "Britain's History and Memory of Transatlantic Slavery: Local Nuances of a 'National Sin,'" *Social History* 42, no. 4 (2017): 555–556, and, Dresser, "Remembering Slavery and Abolition in Bristol," *Slavery and Abolition* 30, no. 2 (2009): 223–246.

245 Elliott Francis, "MLK Comic Book Helped Inspire Arab Spring," *WAMU* (blog), accessed September 30, 2020, https://wamu.org/story/11/08/24/mlk_comic_book_helped_inspire_arab_spring/.

246 "The Bristol Bus Boycott 1963," plaque, Bristol bus station, England, photo by author.

Index